Come to the edge
We might fall
Come to the edge
it's too high
COME TO THE EDGE!
And they came
and he pushed
and they flew ...

Come to the Edge
°Christopher Logue, 1968

Praise for *The Learner's Toolkit*

We want children to learn more than knowledge. They need skills and they need to develop personal qualities. The aptitudes and outlooks they develop will help them to acquire knowledge and to become the sort of people that most of us identify as 'successful'.

Confident, able to bounce back, willing to try, thoughtful, reflective, compassionate, helpful, co-operative...the list goes on...

This book supports the new Secondary Curriculum in its efforts to promote Personal Development and links diversity to the Social Emotional Aspects of Learning (SEAL) Framework for secondary schools. It gives teachers ideas, starting points, plans and examples to help them use their own ideas to support the progress of young people in the most vital of all areas of learning...how to cope with and contribute to the world in which they find themselves.

Mick Waters, Director of Curriculum, QCA

This book turns good intentions into classroom realities.

Jackie Beere has produced a powerful and extensive resource for all of us who want learners to become independent, self-aware, socially skilled and responsible. Surely these qualities are the new, broader 'standards' that the nation is now realising matter over and above examination results.

In tune with the zeitgeist and drawing on established ideas from brain-based learning, accelerated learning, emotional intelligence, citizenship, values education and holistic growth, this book is utterly down-to-earth and packed full of workable strategies. It is written by someone who knows the chalk-face well. Jackie's wisdom and experience shine through in the breadth, novelty and detail of the impressive library of lesson plans.

Cleverly, Jackie has woven together the work of several leading educationalists, combined it with current QCA, National Strategy and Ofsted guidance, and produced a graceful and systematic framework that is translated into enjoyable student-friendly activities complete with in-built thoughts about continuity, progression and assessment. She captures the consensus that is beginning to emerge about the competences and attributes that all learners need – now more than ever. In easy-to-teach chunks, *The Learner's Toolkit* unfolds this modern agenda by using some of the best professional insights of recent years to deliver our new set of national priorities.

Paul Ginnis, Trainer and bestselling author of *The Teacher's Toolkit*

Developed and honed in the cut and thrust of real classrooms, it directly supports the SEAL programme by addressing three core areas – "Emotional Intelligence", "Learning to Learn" and "Values for Life". It's not, though, just a "how to" book for teachers – though that aspect is certainly there. What's specially valuable is the wealth of classroom material that's provided – detailed lessons, with resources that children will find interesting and challenging. You've heard all the rhetoric about emotional intelligence, and the need to create confident learners. Now here's a resource that will help you to do something about it, right now, in your classroom.

Gerald Haigh, former Headteacher, writer and consultant for the Times Educational Supplement and other educational publications

If you are a student - (or a parent wanting to really help a student) - grab this book now. It's written by an outstanding teacher and packed full of practical, easy-to-follow advice that will improve anyone's results. It's all about working smarter - not necessarily harder.

Colin Rose, Founder of Accelerated Learning Systems Ltd

Full of practical ideas to help teachers help pupils to learn how to learn.

Bill Lucas, Chairman, Talent Foundation

This book is a fantastic, innovative resource for learning to learn and implementing SEAL because its not just theory, its got more than fifty planned lessons that you can use directly with students. I have used it as part of my competency based KS3 course. These lessons really work and my favourite are the lessons on emotional intelligence; my students really enjoy making the empathy glasses and the mood monitor.

As I have a leadership role planning competency-based projects I find being able to use these ready made lessons as part of the scheme helps my team deliver high quality learning to learn experiences. Some of the more able kids can actually work through these lessons themselves so parents could use them to develop thinking and learning skills at home.

The photocopiable lessons make this pack great value for creating easy worksheets but just as useful is the DVD with all the lessons on. Using my laptop I can put the lesson up on the whiteboard, saving so much preparation time because all the activities are pre pared. I've heard you can get work books for the kids so that would so useful if you needed students to work through all the lessons themselves or you wanted to save time and money on photocopying.

What I really like about *The Learner's Toolkit* is that it includes everything you need to develop the social and emotional intelligence that students need to be successful and happy at school, in exams and with their friends and family. The brilliant thing about it is that it actually transforms teachers that teach it as well!

Helen Boyle, AST, Campion School, Northants.

I feel thankful to Jackie Beere for bringing together some hope, activities and simple explanations in such a way that I had to read it from cover to cover.

What wonderful ways to learn.

A great little toolkit!

Betty Rudd Education Psychologist

This book definitely supports my view point that academic qualifications are of absolutely no use whatsoever if one leaves school or tertiary education without any basic life skills. The fact that Jackie has looked at how to combine learning of academics and life skills is highly interesting and something I would want to spend time learning more about. I believe the approach she is proposing will have a huge impact on young people's ability to live far better balanced life styles as adults than many adults have done since 'education' became available to the 'masses'.

 Learning about emotional intelligence and the variety of skills that comes under its umbrella is a breath of fresh air for an educational system that has promoted academic learning to the exclusion of learners humanness.

Kathleen Ginn, Author of *The Secret Learning Code*

This is an invaluable resource as schools move more towards equipping youngsters with the knowledge, skills and attributes that they require rather than just the subject content. The aims of education are shifting and this book offers a really good way for schools to focus more on teaching children rather than teaching subjects. Any tutorial programme should have this book as a feature as it is so user-friendly and the resources of such quality.

Overall, an excellent book that already has a permanent place on my desk!

Jon Harris, Assistant Headteacher, Cheslyn Hay Sport and Community High School

The Learner's Toolkit

Supporting the SEAL Framework for Secondary Schools

- Developing Emotional Intelligence
- Instilling Values for Life
- Creating Independent Learners

Jackie Beere

Edited by Ian Gilbert

Crown House Publishing Limited
www.crownhouse.co.uk
www.crownhousepublishing.com

First published by
Crown House Publishing Ltd
Crown Buildings, Bancyfelin, Carmarthen, Wales SA33 5ND, UK
www.crownhouse.co.uk

and

Crown House Publishing Company LLC
6 Trowbridge Drive, Suite 5, Bethel, CT 06801, USA
www.crownhousepublishing.com

© Jackie Beere 2007
Illustrations © Les Evans 2007

First published 2007. Reprinted 2007, 2008 and 2010

British Library of Cataloguing-in-Publication Data
A catalogue entry for this book is available from the British Library.

13-digit ISBN 978-184590070-0
10-digit ISBN 1845900707

LCCN 2007925537

The author and publisher gratefully acknowledge the permission granted to reproduce the copyright material in this book.

Every effort has been made to trace copyright holders and to obtain their permission for the use of copyright material. The publisher apologises for any errors or omissions and would be grateful if notified of any corrections that should be incorporated in future reprints or editions of this book.

The 8Way Thinking Tool (page 58) has been reproduced with the permission of Independent Thinking Ltd.

'The Tyger' by William Blake has been reproduced with the permission of Harper Collins.

Edited by Ian Gilbert

Printed and bound in the UK by *Bell & Bain Ltd, Glasgow.*

Acknowledgements

This book has been inspired by the students of Campion School, who have been my guinea pigs for many of these lessons and always taught me so much. I would like to acknowledge the innovative work of the RSA, in encouraging me to believe that the skills and competencies developed here are as important as subjects. In addition, I have appreciated working with my friends and colleagues at Independent Thinking, especially Ian Gilbert, who make me want to be as good as them at what I do. Thanks also to my friend and mentor Steph Coleman, who teaches me so much from the world outside education.

We would like to thank Connect Publications for permission to update lesson ideas first printed in The Key Stage 3 Learning Kit.

This book is to help kids who didn't have the endless years of grounding in life skills and philosophy that I was given by my mum and dad. Finally, as ever, my love and thanks to my husband, John, and daughters, Lucy and Carrie, who provide the feedback and make me believe I can do anything!

Health warning

The ideas in this book about the brain are based on various research sources and what is helpful in the classroom. Some are controversial and disputed. However, please consider them as metaphors and helpful tools for learning rather than as definitive facts. As a teacher, I have found these ideas to be invaluable in helping children to understand themselves as learners.

Contents

contents

Foreword

Ian Gilbert

Being happy is not something to be left to chance. Self motivation is not a quirk of our genes. Knowing thyself is not just for philosophers. Being a quick and confident learner isn't only the domain of 'clever' students. All of these things can be taught to young people in schools and, as the UK government has finally realised with its Social and Emotional Aspects of Learning (SEAL) programme, *should* be taught in schools.

Let's make one thing clear before you start reaching for the pen to contact the Daily Mail letters page. What we're not talking about is touchy-feely, hippy-trippy, happy-clappy, mumbo-jumbo where we sit in a circle and attempt astral flight to the land where the peonies grow. As governments and businesses around the world are realising, there is a clear educational and economic benefit in having young people and adults who know how to be confident, capable and happy, both as learners and as human beings.

For those of us who experienced a carefree and relatively idyllic childhood (still the majority of us fortunately in the UK) here are some statistics to make your heart bleed:

- The UK has one of the highest rates of self harm in Europe, at 400 per 100,000 population, and with suicide the most common cause of death in men under the age of 35[1]

- One in ten children between the ages of one and 15 has a mental health disorder[2]

- Estimates vary, but research suggests that 20% of children have a mental health problem in any given year, and about 10% at any one time[3]

- Rates of mental health problems among children increase as they reach adolescence. Disorders affect 10.4% of boys aged 5–10, rising to 12.8% of boys aged 11–15; and 5.9% of girls aged 5–10, rising to 9.6% of girls aged 11–15[4]

- Young people who are misusing drugs or alcohol have the highest risk of death by suicide[5]

- By 2020 depression will be the second largest killer after heart disease – and studies show that depression is a contributory factor to fatal coronary disease[6]

1. The National Service Framework For Mental Health – Five Years On, Department Of Health (2005)
2. The Office for National Statistics Mental health in children and young people in Great Britain (2005)
3. Lifetime Impacts: Childhood and Adolescent Mental Health, Understanding The Lifetime Impacts, Mental Health Foundation (2005)
4. Mental Disorder More Common In Boys, National Statistics Online (2004)
5. *Mental Health and Growing Up* – Royal College of Psychiatrists (2004)
6. World Health Organisation report on mental illness (2001)

■ Estimates indicate that self-reported work-related stress, depression or anxiety account for an estimated 10.5 million reported lost working days per year in Britain[7]

■ A Unicef study involving 21 developed countries showed that British children were the least satisfied with their lives, whilst the World Health Organisation predicts that childhood psychiatric disorders will rise by 50 per cent by 2020.[8]

If we want young people to become happy and effective adults who can make and sustain meaningful relationships, who can deal with change, failure and success, who can motivate themselves from the inside, who can learn, forget what they've learned because it's all changed and then re-learn, and who aspire to be all they can be (and be happy with what they are regardless) then we must send young people away from us with the skills and competence to achieve all this.

And if yours is an academically successful school where children leave with a raft of top-notch grades, maybe it is in your head that the alarm bells should be ringing the loudest. According to clinical psychologist Oliver James, there are studies that show that it is high-achieving girls who are especially at risk from the effects of low self-esteem and its consequent effects.[9]

On top of all this, recent brain research about the need for positive emotions for effective learning (type 'dopamine and learning' into your favourite search engine and you'll see) backs up what Plato told us over two thousand years ago:

'All learning has an emotional base.'

Having emotionally intelligent and balanced children is one thing but that's not enough to prepare them for the speed of change and scale of challenge they will face beyond school. One of the best selling books of this century so far is *The World is Flat* by Pulitzer-prize winning writer Thomas Friedman. He states that 'knowing how to "learn how to learn"' will be *the* critical skill for the 21st century:

7. Stress-related and psychological disorders, Health and Safety Executive (2007) Please note that in this document it is also pointed out that 'occupation and industry groups containing teachers and nurses, along with professional and managerial groups particularly those in the public sector have high prevalence rates of work-related stress...' So feel free to use the resources in this book on yourself and your colleagues too!
8. Children 'need lessons in happiness' Telegraph.co.uk (2007)
9. Britain on the Couch: Why We're Unhappier Compared with 1950, Despite Being Richer – A Treatment for the Low-serotonin Society, Oliver James (1998)

'The more we push out the boundaries of knowledge and technology, the more complex tasks that machines can do, the more those with specialised education, or the ability to learn how to learn, will be in demand, and for better pay.'[10]

The days of spoon-feeding for exam results have got to be numbered if we, in education, are going to do the job that society needs us to do.

(This is also echoed by our universities where a recent report states that '… narrow accountability based on exam success and league tables … leads to spoon feeding … Learners who may have achieved academic success at A Level … struggle to cope with the more independent and self-directed style of learning expected by higher education tutors.' The report goes on to point out that 'Valuable time is lost at the beginning of HE courses developing independent learning skills that should have been developed, at least to an extent, already.'[11])

Furthermore, it's not even a question of, 'Well, *how* do you do all this?' We know how. Teaching children how to learn is finally taking off in many schools now (although I am still asked the question, 'Should we be teaching children how to learn then?' to which the only response is 'Do grandads suck Polos?!') and there are schools giving children lessons in how to be happy, most notably the prestigious Wellington College in Berkshire.[12]

So it's not *how* but rather, 'How come you haven't started yet?'

Fortunately, with this *Learner's Toolkit* in your hands, you have all you need to get going straightaway.

In this resource you will find everything necessary to introduce students to virtually every aspect of 21st century learning from knowing your EQ from your IQ, handling stress and fear and understanding yourself better as a learner to improving your memory, controlling your moods and training your amazing brain.

10. *The World is Flat: The Globalized World in the Twenty-first Century*, Thomas Friedman, (2006)
11. Nuffield Review Higher Education Focus Groups Preliminary Report, Wilde et al, (2006)
12. Pupils to have a key to happiness, BBC News Online (2007) http://news.bbc.co.uk/1/hi/education/4915714.stm

Drawing as it does from Jackie's first book *The Key Stage 3 Learning Kit* (although greatly expanded and developed) the exercises in this book have already proven their worth with many schools around the country. Part of their success is that they draw on Jackie's unique experience as a teacher, an Advanced Skills Teacher, a headteacher, a School Improvement Partner, an advisor to government, a Master NLP Practitioner, a lecturer, a speaker, an author, a freelance consultant, and someone who for over a decade has been at the forefront of 21st century educational theory and practice.

This resource is a goldmine of hundreds of simple and enjoyable ideas and exercises, but the effect they have when delivered well has repercussions way beyond the classroom and into the future.

The head of Wellington College is quoted as saying, 'To me, the most important job of any school is to turn out young men and women who are happy and secure – more important than the latest bulletin from the Department for Education about whatever.'

This book not only echoes those sentiments fully but also gives you many proven strategies and techniques to make this possible. I know that as you make the shift from teaching subjects to teaching children, you will find it a most invaluable tool.

Ian Gilbert
Suffolk
July 2007

Introduction

The secondary SEAL resources, are to be launched nationally in September ... it catches a tide of separate waves in education, including circle time, emotional literacy, anger management, behaviour improvement and monitoring of learning ... schools welcome official blessings to concentrate on what they have always considered to be the core values – co-operation, self esteen and consideration for others ... and learning!

Gerald Haigh, TES, 1st June 2007

The Learner's Toolkit is a comprehensive set of resources that will help teachers implement the SEAL (Social and Emotional aspects of Learning) programme recommended by the National Strategy. It is divided into three sections: Emotional Intelligence, Learning to Learn and Values for Life. These sections target the aims of QCA's 21st century curriculum for Successful Learners, Confident Individuals and Responsible Citizens. The lessons in this toolkit will provide detailed plans that enable schools to transform learning and raise standards through impacting on personal and emotional development. In addition, this toolkit creates resources to develop the crucial habits and dispositions stated in the Ofsted 2020 vision document which include:

- *taking responsibility for, and being able to manage one's own learning and developing the habits of effective learning*

- *knowing how to work independently without close supervision*

- *being confident and able to investigate problems and find solutions*

- *being resilient in the face of difficulties*

- *being creative, inventive, enterprising and entrepreneurial.*

Ofsted Vision 2020, 2007

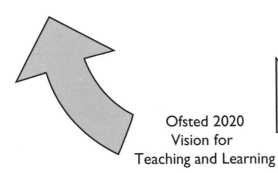

National Strategy Programme
for Social and Emotional
Intelligence (SEAL)

QCA 21st century curriculum
Successful Learners
Confident Individuals
Responsible Citizens

Ofsted 2020
Vision for
Teaching and Learning

The three sections overlap in many aspects and reinforce each other in many ways. There are more than 50 lessons written to last up to one hour and each lesson has a full set of teacher's notes with guidance on how to deliver the lesson. Pages can be copied and shared with students.

EQ – essential lessons in how to manage your mind and emotions

L2L – all about the brain and how to use it

Values – lessons that reinforce personal values

These themes are linked to QCA aims for successful learners, confident individuals and responsible citizens.

This toolkit can be used for PSHE lessons, Citizenship lessons, Learning to Learn lessons, or as part of a competency based curriculum. It can be used across KS3 and into KS4 or KS2. The lessons are planned to develop important competencies that many employers say are vital for success at work and at home. These competencies include:

The competencies	Teaching strategies
Communication and collaboration	Encourage group work, team building and leadership skills. Formal and informal speaking and presentations, as well as high quality writing outcomes.
Learning to learn	Focus on how we are learning. Use a language for describing learning styles and preferences.
Investigation and enquiry	Asking high level questions and students learning to ask high level questions. Focus on enquiry based learning.
Creativity and enterprise	Trying out ideas, developing own content and independent learning. Encourage taking risks and learning through mistakes.
Self-management	Managing their own learning, working to dealines and taking responsibility for outcomes. Using self and peer assessment strategies to develop self awareness and confidence.

Using this book to deliver a competency based curriculum

Each lesson provides strategies for developing competencies and dispositions that are crucial to independent learning. Students should be encouraged to self assess in order to develop their skills and there are two grids that may help with this. The grids create a framework for assessing progress and a picture of what students are working towards. We need to be able to answer the question, 'What does good progress look like and how do we know when we have improved?'

Assessment Tool 1

This grid helps locate lessons related to a particular competency. The competencies shown are adapted from the Royal Society of Arts competencies and should be seen as just one possible set. You may wish to use all or some of these competencies, but schools should choose their own set that suits their context.

Students may wish to assess themselves against some of these criteria when they have completed lessons or they may wish to add alternative statements to the grid. It should be used as a flexible live document that monitors progress and learning.

Competency	Section 1 – EQ	Section 2 – L2L	Section 3 – Values
Communication and collaboration	1, 2, 3, 4, 6, 7, 13, 14, 20, 21,	25, 32, 34, 40	43, 44, 45, 46, 48, 49, 50, 51, 52
Learning to learn	2, 3, 6, 8, 10, 13, 15, 16, 17, 18, 21	24–41(all)	47, 50
Investigation and enquiry	13, 14, 15, 16, 17, 18, 21	27, 28, 30, 31, 32, 33, 37, 38	42, 43, 50
Creativity and enterprise	5, 6, 7, 10, 13, 14, 16, 18	24, 25, 26, 30, 36, 37, 40, 41	44, 47, 48, 50
Self management	1–23 (all)	24–41(all)	44, 45, 46, 48, 50, 52

CLICrS – Competency assessment form

	Communication and collaboration	Learning to learn	Investigation and inquiry	Creativity and enterprise	Self management/emotional intelligence
LEVEL 1	Reluctant to communicate beyond immediate peers. Find effective group work challenging.	Not aware of learning style and how to develop it. Finds traditional learning difficult. Fails to engage with tasks. Seeks immediate gratification.	Accepts sources without question. Needs support to ask the right questions. Finds summarising ideas difficult.	Needs prompting to take initiative. Finds creating ideas challenging.	Lacks self awareness. Disorganised. Fails to take personal responsibility for outcomes.

CLICrS – Competency assessment form

	Communication and collaboration	Learning to learn	Investigation and inquiry	Creativity and enterprise	Self management/emotional intelligence
LEVEL 2	Can take part in group work and is developing leadership skills. Can communicate orally and in writing at a satisfactory level. Has level of empathy and respect for others.	Knows learning profile. Is interested in learning. Needs some support but will work independently. Is developing strategies to transfer skills from one context to another.	Asks questions when prompted. Can summarise an argument and pick out the important points.	Willing to try out new ideas. Will tackle challenges with support. Within group will create solutions.	Learns from mistakes. High self esteem. Confident self belief. Well organised and effective. Manages anxiety and challenges very well.
LEVEL 3	An excellent leader or participator. Excellent communication skills, orally in writing and multimedia. Can gain rapport with peers or others quickly and effectively. Demonstrates and sustains respect and empathy to a high level.	Understands learning styles and is continuously learning. Has flexible approaches to learning. Can learn independently and coach others. Can transfer skills from one context to another. Is comfortable with making mistakes and learning from experience.	Can interrogate resources and summarise messages. Can question very effectively. Can complete a critique on a proposal or project.	Is capable of thinking of highly creative solutions. Can take initiative and tackle challenges with flair and originality. Is open to new ideas and experiences.	Organises time and resources highly effectively. High level of self esteem and intrapersonal intelligence. High level of self awareness. Can manage anxiety and stress effectively. Can motivate themselves and others. Has ambitious goals. Can gain excellent rapport with a variety of audiences.

Assessment Tool 2

This assessment tool helps to identify some levels of working that demonstrate effective learning. It is not definitive and 'mastery' encompasses a wide spectrum of ambitions for learning that will continue for life. 'Mastery' of learning is a condition we aim for and continually work towards. If students can understand what it is they are aiming for, it is more likely they will see the point of the lessons and make a connection with the aims of the lessons.

This audit can be used in lesson observations (by teachers and students) to see which behaviours are demonstrated. It can also be used in target setting meetings with students when they can discuss where they fit into the levels of competence. The aim will be that as students move through the programme, they achieve ever higher levels of competence.

Student Learning to Learn Audit

Typical traits	Working towards (developing)	Working at (competent)	Working beyond (mastery)
Confident individuals *(EQ)* Communication Self belief Self awareness Self management Interpersonal skills	Overcoming low self esteem. Increasing self awareness regarding skills and abilities. Effectively organising time and resources. Working effectively with others.	Able to learn from mistakes with support. Aware of abilities and skills and able to use them most of the time. Can organise time to complete most tasks to deadline. Communicates well with peers. Can concentrate and apply themselves to … Willing to try out ideas and hypothesise. Uses resources well.	Learns from mistakes. High self esteem. Confident self belief. Well organised and effective. Manages anxiety and challenges very well. Can gain excellent rapport with a variety of audiences. Sustained concentration and commitment. Enthusiastic and energetic. Adaptable and flexible.

Typical traits	Working towards (developing)	Working at (competent)	Working beyond (mastery)
Successful learners *(Learning to learn)* Communication Enquiry Creativity Independence Resilience Persistence Engagement	Finding out about themselves as a learner. Supporting their own learning. Avoiding giving up too easily. Developing curiosity. Trying new ideas. Relying on the teacher for confidence. Improving communication. Avoiding distraction.	Knows learning profile. Is interested in learning. Willing to try out new ideas. Needs some support but will work independently. Asks questions when prompted. Can communicate orally and in writing at a satisfactory level. Can deal with frustration. Uses time well. Monitors own learning.	Knows learning profile and extends/applies it consistently. Excellent communicator. Produces many creative ideas. Able to work on own initiative. Never gives up but continues to try new approaches. Asks difficult questions and challenges concepts. Low dependence on teacher. Sets targets and monitors them. Independent learner who uses initiative.
Responsible Citizens *(Values)* Communication Participation Enterprise and initiative Global awareness Prepared for work Respect and integrity	Active participation. Increasing motivation to complete work tasks or get involved in teamwork. Improving communication in a respectful way to others or demonstrate empathy or tolerance. Increasing awareness or regarding global issues. Considering future working life.	Will participate in activity. Can make a good contribution to a team. Sometimes produces good ideas. Has a sensitivity to global issues and international awareness. Respects others and can be trusted. Has goals for future working life. Knows when to work alone or with others.	Flexible as leader or participator in a group and will make the group have a successful outcome. Is conscious of sustainable solutions and international issues. Demonstrates self respect and tolerance, empathy and respect for others. Has the confidence to generate enterprise ideas and follow them through. Has goals and ambitions for working life. Can coach others.

Lessons that will deliver each of these competencies are shown here:

Competence	Section 1 Lessons:	Section 2 Lessons:	Section 3 Lessons:
Confident Individuals	1–24	26, 37, 38, 41	44, 48, 50
Successful Learners	5, 9, 11, 12, 14, 15, 16, 17, 18, 19, 22	26–41	44, 47, 48, 50, 52
Responsible Citizens	1–7, 15, 17, 18, 19, 20, 21, 24	27, 35, 41	42–52

The Habits of Emotional Intelligence

Aims

This section is based around the 10 Habits of Emotional Intelligence (EQ).

Emotional intelligence encompasses the self-awareness and self-management skills which lead to confidence, tolerance and success. Emotional intelligence combines interpersonal and intrapersonal intelligence and leads to the development of expert communication skills. (From the Howard Gardner Multiple Intelligences model.)

Can we help young people develop the qualities of personality that will enable them to overcome difficulties and become successful and happy? The world that our children grow up in has increasing demands for flexibility, risk taking and enterprise set against a culture of blame and litigation. Being emotionally intelligent means throwing off the victim culture and taking responsibility for creating your own future. The qualities of emotional intelligence such as resilience, optimism and empathy are ways of thinking and seeing the world that should become unconscious habits. The first step towards developing these habits is to understand their importance and then rehearse the thoughts and feelings which cultivate them. This set of lessons is the first stage in 'learning how to learn' and can be used with students throughout all age ranges.

EQ	Habit	Lesson
1.	Take responsibility for yourself	1, 2, 3, 4
2.	Create goals for life	5
3.	Have confidence and self-belief	6, 7, 8
4.	Be persistent and resilient	9
5.	Be an optimist	10, 11
6.	Take care of yourself – body and brain	12, 13, 14, 15, 16
7.	Practise self-discipline and willpower	17
8.	Have courage	18, 19, 20
9.	Co-operate and communicate	21, 22
10.	Prioritise and plan	23

Before you teach this section know that you will probably have to learn how to be a role model for EQ yourself. In teaching this section you will need to investigate your own habits and be a learner as well as a teacher!

Each lesson includes a 'first thoughts' starter and most include an extension activity. Lessons are planned to last 50 minutes to one hour. Plenaries can be added to review learning.

The aim of these lessons is to help students understand what EQ is and how it works. The self-assessment exercise is worth doing for yourself and for setting some of your own targets.

25 lessons in EQ

1. Understanding Emotional Intelligence (EQ)
2. Test your EQ
3. Get to know your best friend – YOU
4. It's MY life
5. Goals for life
6. Build your confidence
7. Be your own life coach
8. Mind Power
9. Persistence and Resilience
10. Mood Control
11. Optimism
12. Taking care of mind and body
13. Stress Management
14. Thinking skills
15. Asking the right questions
16. Mastering your memory
17. Train your brain to wait
18. Having courage to think in other ways – Thinking hats
19. Grow your confidence and courage
20. Courage – be brave
21. Empathy – put yourself in other's shoes
22. Communicate and co-operate for success
23. Prioritise and plan
24. Review the habits of EQ
25. What have you learnt about EQ

teacher's notes

EQ matters more than IQ...

'Emotional Intelligence is a master aptitude that profoundly affects all other abilities'.

Daniel Goleman

Emotional intelligence is knowing and understanding yourself well and having ways of thinking that make you self-confident and good at forming positive relationships with others. By developing your Emotional Intelligence you will be both happy and successful at whatever you do.

LESSON 1

Understanding Emotional Intelligence (EQ)

(Please note that EQ stands for 'emotional quotient'– in this EQ pack means the same as emotional intelligence)

Resources

A4 size card folded in half. Many coloured pens, pencils.

Aim

By the end of this lesson students will understand what we mean by EQ and how it can help create successful outcomes.

First thoughts

Discussion of what qualities successful people have and how they relate to behaviours.

Understand each characteristic of EQ by talking through the top ten habits. Students make an EQ card that makes each habit easy to remember and practice.

The card will be something they can take home and keep, so it should be colourful and include pictures and words.

Slogans should be memorable, rhyming, silly, clever – anything that works.

Review

Go round the class reading out the students' slogans and guessing which EQ habit they work for.

> People will forget what you said,
> people will forget what you did,
> but people will never forget
> the way you made them feel.

teacher's notes

Understanding Emotional Intelligence (EQ)

The Habits of Emotional Intelligence

A habit is something you do frequently and unconsciously. You may always sit on the same chair or use the same mug at home. You may always wear your clothes in a certain way or always listen to the same kind of music. Many of your habits develop in your unconscious mind and they just feel comfortable and become part of you.

> You have good habits and bad habits and they are *very* important in defining who you are.
>
> What are your good habits? _____
> For example, eating fruit every day.
>
> What are your bad habits? _____
> For example, staying up too late.

Habit 1:
Take responsibility for yourself

If you do things on a regular basis they become habits and can shape your life. For example, if you are *always* late for everything it could cost you a good job.

Habits of EQ can make you successful.

However brainy you are you will only be successful if you are EMOTIONALLY intelligent

Each lesson will help you develop the 10 EQ habits

This is all about controlling your emotions and the way you think to make them work in a positive way for you. The emotional part of the brain is right in the centre of all brain activity. This type of intelligence relates to your SELF SMART and PEOPLE SMART scores which are discussed in Section 2.

● Find out in this section if *you* are already emotionally intelligent.

● Find out how to improve your EQ so that you can be a winner.

● Find out how to develop the habits of EQ so that you don't even have to think about them.

There are some people that succeed in life and there are others that don't. Some scientists now believe that there are characteristics that are even more important than your IQ or intelligence in determining whether *you* will be a success in life.

Understanding Emotional Intelligence (EQ)

EQ. The top ten habits

1. **Take responsibility for yourself** – don't blame others, don't make excuses, know that only you can change your life.

2. **Create goals for life** – have a goal and take action to get to it.

3. **Have confidence and self-belief** – know your strengths and work on your weaknesses. Be kind to yourself and know you can be brilliant.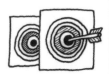

4. **Be persistent and resilient** – never give up, see every mistake as a learning experience.

5. **Be an optimist** – always look for the positive. Smile, be cheerful and look to the future.

6. **Take care of yourself** – sleep, eat and exercise well. Keep growing your brain by learning something new.

7. **Practice self-discipline and willpower** – train yourself to wait for things.

8. **Have courage** – get out of your comfort zone and do something different and scary every day.

9. **Co-operate and communicate** – take every opportunity to support others and work together.

10. **Prioritise and plan** – make lists of what you need to do and take control.

Understanding Emotional Intelligence (EQ)

TASK

Create an EQ card with slogans for each of the top ten habits. Here are some ideas to get you started:

Persistence
'If at first you don't succeed, try, try, try again'.

Willpower
'No pain, no gain'.

Goals for life
'If you can dream it, you can do it'.

TIP: Make the card colourful and full of pictures and varying fonts. This will help your brain remember the slogans.

PERSISTENCE
'If at first you don't succeed, try, try, try again'.

Willpower
'No pain, no gain'.

Goals for life
'If you can dream it, you can do it'.

Test your EQ

Habit 1: Take responsibility for yourself

Have you got what it takes to be a winner?

Aim

To be aware of strengths and weaknesses and to set targets for improvement.

Explain the test – giving examples for each question. Encourage students to use the full range of marking (scores 1–5).

It is important for friends to do the test on each other in order to check out the results. Please treat the scores with a sense of healthy scepticism as they are a self-assessment. However, these definitions may amuse students.

Score 40+	You are an emotional genius!
Score 30+	A good score but some areas to work on
Score 20+	You need to work on your emotional development
Under 20	Trouble ahead!

Choose the 3 lowest scores and set targets for the Students can note action required and slogans that will help them, such as in the example given.

As part of the review all students can verbalise their targets which will help confirm their commitment to them.

Teacher's Extension Task

Read 'Emotional Intelligence – why it matters more than IQ' by Daniel Goleman.

Test your EQ

Have you got what it takes to be a winner?

Habit 1:
Take responsibility for yourself

EQ is more important than brainpower in determining whether you will be a success in school and in life. Test yourself…

Mark each quality up to five according to how much you feel it applies to you.

	Low				High
1. Do you take responsibility for your own life?	1	2	3	4	5
2. Do you have goals and dreams for the future?	1	2	3	4	5
3. Have you got confidence and self-belief?	1	2	3	4	5
4. Are you persistent – or do you give up easily?	1	2	3	4	5
5. Are you an optimist that sees the positive side of things?	1	2	3	4	5
6. Do you take care of your health and fitness?	1	2	3	4	5
7. Do you have willpower and self-discipline?	1	2	3	4	5
8. Have you got the courage to try new things?	1	2	3	4	5
9. Do you work well with others and listen carefully to them?	1	2	3	4	5
10. Are you good at planning and organising your work?	1	2	3	4	5

Five is very high, one is very low. Try to be honest.

Test your EQ

Ask your friend/partner if they agree with your self scoring and discuss your answers.

You **can** improve your EQ – and become a winner.

Choose your 3 lowest scores.

_____

_____

_____

1
2
3

Create a target sheet that plans
the way you will improve your EQ.

like this example

**Understanding
your strengths and
weaknesses will
help you succeed**

The Learner's Toolkit © Jackie Beere and Crown House Publishing Ltd

Test your EQ

Example Target Sheet for growing my EQ

EQ Target	Action needed to develop better habits	Slogans and sayings that will help motivate me
1. Take responsibility for your own life.	No excuses. Accept responsibility. Review where I am and where I want to be. Don't blame anyone else. Make a plan and monitor it every week. Don't be afraid to make mistakes and learn from them.	If it's to be, it's up to me. If I can dream it, I can do it. I can't control what happens but I can control how I think about it.
2. Be brave, take risks.	Give myself little challenges to do things that scare me. Walk a different way to school. Make a new friend. Eat a different food or watch a different television programme. Volunteer for a club or presentation that I wouldn't normally do. Say yes to a request for help.	Do something that scares me every day. If it doesn't kill you it makes you stronger. Every mistake is a learning experience.
3. Get organised – prioritise and plan.	Make lists every day of what you need to do and tick them off as you do them. Check your bag is packed with all the right stuff. Use your phone to remind you of deadlines and times of important events. Avoid displacement activity, such as phoning mates or surfing the net to avoid doing unpleasant jobs.	Do the worst first. Work smarter, not harder.
1.		
2.		
3.		

LESSON 3

Get to know your best friend – YOU

Habit 1: Take responsibility for yourself

Resources

Large paper (sugar paper) and pens.

Aims

To become aware of how the unconscious mind works to create beliefs and behaviours.

First thoughts

■ Talk about the unconscious mind and how much of our thinking comes from here. Get students to think of their conscious mind as an iceberg with the voices they hear and the sights they see at any moment as the top bit, which their conscious mind is aware of. They can switch conscious focus to other things such as their feet, their bottoms on seats, or the noises outside at any time.

■ Use questions to explore student reactions and reflect on how they control emotions.

■ Answers to the questions can be written down in a book or on a whiteboard and shared with a partner.

■ Students find it very hard to learn from criticism without letting it affect their self-esteem. This is worth a discussion.

■ The core of the lesson is what they learn about themselves from these thoughts.

■ The extension task to investigate beliefs and values is an opportunity to find out who has influenced their views. These questions could take up a whole lesson if a Community of Enquiry structure is used. (See Glossary).

Time for a brain booster session (Lesson 30).

Top tip

If possible play the song 'The greatest love of all' by George Benson and discuss the lyrics.

Students are more likely to understand the way teachers try to get them to improve their performance if they role-play, "student" and "form-tutor".

Review

Spend two minutes in silence thinking about what you have learnt about yourself in this lesson.

Extension

Write a letter to yourself.

teacher's notes

Section 1 • The Habits of Emotional Intelligence

Get to know your best friend – YOU

Self-awareness: How does your mind work?

Control your thinking and your inner voice to get what you want in life. Start by understanding how you work. Many of your thoughts and feelings come from your unconscious mind. This diagram is based on the Freudian theory of mind.

Habit 1:

Take responsibility for yourself

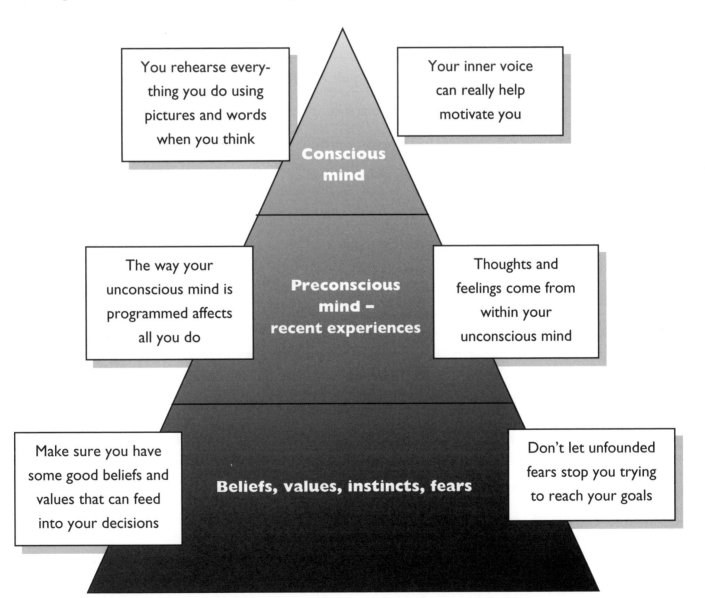

You rehearse every-thing you do using pictures and words when you think

Your inner voice can really help motivate you

Conscious mind

The way your unconscious mind is programmed affects all you do

Thoughts and feelings come from within your unconscious mind

Preconscious mind – recent experiences

Make sure you have some good beliefs and values that can feed into your decisions

Don't let unfounded fears stop you trying to reach your goals

Beliefs, values, instincts, fears

This lesson will help develop your *INTRAPERSONAL* intelligence.
Just thinking about the questions on the next page will help you understand your unconscious mind and help you learn to take more control of your thinking.

Get to know your best friend – YOU

The aim of this lesson is to help you get to know yourself better. It takes courage to be honest about yourself so decide now whether you are brave enough!

Look at these questions and consider your answers carefully.

1.	What do you do when you are angry?
2.	What makes you feel sad?
3.	When was the last time you laughed out loud? When was the last time you cried?
4.	Think of three things that you like to do and consider why.
5.	Who would you talk to if you had a major worry?
6.	How well do you cope when someone criticises you?
7.	How do you cheer yourself up if you are in a bad mood?
8.	When was the last time you couldn't get your way about something important? What did you do?
9.	What do you do when you get stuck at school?
10.	How would you describe your personality?

Discuss your answers with your partner and see if they agree or disagree with you.

Choose some of your answers. Write them down and put them in an envelope.
Pass them to another pair and ask them to write down the questions they relate to.
Then discuss as a foursome and see how many you got right.

What 3 things have you learnt about yourself from this?

1. _____

2. _____

3. _____

If you didn't learn anything that says something about you too!

Get to know your best friend – YOU

This is most important thing you will do today!

Think of a positive thing to say to yourself every day when you look in the mirror. Write it down. Say it aloud. Say it in your head. Louder.

Give it a kind, lovely voice. Say it again.
Say it every day. Mean it!

Extension task

BELIEFS AND VALUES – use these questions to investigate your beliefs and values...

1. Write down three things you believe are important for anyone to be happy.

_____

_____

_____

2. If you won £1 million what would you spend it on?

_____

_____

_____

3. What qualities do you value in a friend?

_____

_____

_____

Now ask three other people of different ages for their answers and compare them with your own.
Report the results of your survey to the rest of your class.

It's MY life

Habit 1: Take responsibility for your self

Aim

To make students decide to take more responsibility for their outcomes and to avoid the 'victim' culture.

First thoughts

How much are *you* in control? This examines what things you can and can't control.

This could be the most powerful lesson of all.

The purpose of this lesson is to help students understand that they are in control of their lives and that whatever happens to them they have choice in how they react to it. This is very empowering. It is the opposite of the 'victim culture' that blames others. The starter investigates the obvious things that are within and out of their control. The story demonstrates that it is not what you have but what you make of it that matters.

The following activities give students an opportunity to investigate how they could react in various ways to situations.

The magic formula could be developed into a poster for display around school.

> If it's to be, it's up to me.

It's MY life

There is only one person that is responsible for your happiness – YOU!

Habit 1:

Take responsibility for yourself

First thoughts

Add at **LEAST** three more things to each list.

Out of my control	In my control
Name	Attitude
Family	Friends
Looks?	

1. _____	1. _____
2. _____	2. _____
3. _____	3. _____
4. _____	4. _____
5. _____	5. _____
6. _____	6. _____

You may have found out that making two lists is not simple because some things are in both columns. You can influence anything that happens to you because it is how you *respond* to things that makes the difference.

It's MY life

True Story

Once there was a girl called Alison, who was born with no arms and no legs because of a birth defect caused by a drug taken by her mother during pregnancy. Her hands were attached to her torso. On the same day a beautiful, healthy baby boy was born into a wealthy, caring family. Alison became a famous artist and sculptor, campaigning for the rights of disabled people and immortalised forever through a huge statue in Trafalgar Square. The boy went to the best schools but became de-motivated and involved in crime in his teenage years. He was dead by the time he was 25, leaving his family devastated at the waste of life.

Group work

Why do some people have everything and lose it?

How do some people who have obstacles to overcome make something wonderful of their lives? Discuss in groups stories of success and failure.

Task: **Think of 20 excuses for not doing your homework/coursework**

1. _____

2. _____

3. _____

4. _____

5. _____

6. _____

7. _____

8. _____

9. _____

10. _____

11. _____

12. _____

13. _____

14. _____

15. _____

16. _____

17. _____

18. _____

19. _____

20. _____

Think of 5 reasons not to make excuses

1. _____

2. _____

3. _____

4. _____

5. _____

'99% of all failures come from people who have a habit of making excuses'

It's MY life

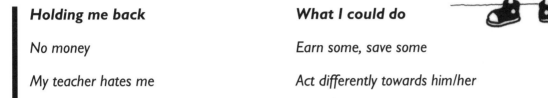

Now think of 3 things that hold you back from being successful or happy.
For each one write down what you could do to change the situation.

For example:

Holding me back	**What I could do**
No money	Earn some, save some
My teacher hates me	Act differently towards him/her
....	....
....	....
....	....

Magic formula:
Stuff happens + You react = Outcome

Give up all your excuses and take
100% responsibility for your life!

The only thing you can change in the magic formula
is your reaction.
Your actions include how you THINK about something
and especially your attitude.
Try it, change your reaction and see if it changes the
outcome.

Role Play: You arrive home late, your parents are
waiting up, very angry.
Try two scenarios, one where you react
aggressively and one where you react differently.

**If you always
do what you have always
done – you always get
what you always got.**

LESSON 5

Goals for life

| Habit 2: Create goals for life

Resources

Lined paper.

Aim

By the end of this lesson students will understand how important it is to have long-term and short-term goals in life and will have set some!

The emphasis here is to practise creating a very positive picture. Mental rehearsals are something we all do on a regular basis. If we can teach students to mentally rehearse in a positive manner it will make a real difference to their attitude, outlook and achievement.

First thoughts

Students can think of famous people, write them down and then share them with partners or the class. Discussion follows on each one – How did they do it?

The Roger Bannister story emphasises the self-belief factor in goal setting. You may have other stories to offer too.

Do some brain boosters here from Lesson 30.

The second part of the lesson is to focus on creating their own future.

The role-play task involves empathy and checks out the future they have created for themselves.

Review

Why do we need goals?

Extension

Write their goals on a poster for their bedroom wall.

teacher's notes

Goals for life

If you don't know where you are going you will never get there

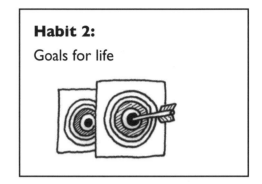

Habit 2:

Goals for life

The most powerful habit for success is *setting yourself goals* and … *believing you can achieve them.*

All in the mind …

Nobody believed that anyone could run the 4 minute mile. It was said to be physically impossible. Roger Bannister succeeded where millions had failed. The next year 37 more runners broke the record. How did Roger Bannister achieve the "impossible"?

First thoughts

Think of five famous and successful people.

1. _____

2. _____

3. _____

4. _____

5. _____

Goals for life

What have they all got in common?

They have achieved their goals.

How did they do it?

1. They had a goal

2. They believed they could achieve it

3. They used strategies that worked to achieve their goals

If they can do it *you* can do it … but first you have to set yourself short-term and long-term goals and think about how you will set about achieving them.

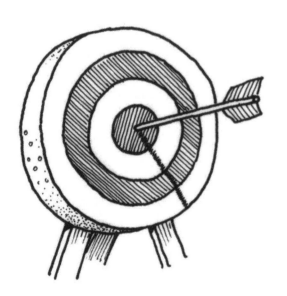

My long-term goal is …

First step
Today I will …

I will achieve this by …

Goals for life

The time to start working towards your goals is *now*.

Simply by writing down and committing to a goal you make a new and important connection in the brain.

A part of the brain lights up whenever a challenge or goal is created.

Create three important goals for this year.

1. _____

2. _____

3. _____

Create two for the next five years.

1. _____

2. _____

What short-term goals do you need to think of for each?

Write a paragraph describing your life as you would like it to be when you are 30 years old. Write it in the present tense.

_____

_____

_____

_____

_____

_____

_____

TASK

Interview your partner as a 30-year-old, talking about their school life and how they achieved

Extension task:

At home, research the lives of your heroes and how they achieved success.

LESSON 6

Build your confidence

Habit 3: Have confidence and self-belief

Build your confidence – believe in yourself.

Build your confidence – with a little help from your friends.

Aim

To build self confidence and peer coaching skill. It is important that students know how to build their confidence explicitly.

All students want confidence, so the starter considers what the external signs of confidence are and gets students to measure themselves.

The main task of the lesson is to consider what is great about themselves and what they need to work on, using peer support and coaching. Pair up people who will help each other to discover the positives and challenge each other with ideas for improvement.

Another opportunity is to get both to assess each other as life coaches and pull out the skills that life coaches should have. For example – listening, encouraging, probing and so on.

The final task is to try to get inside the head of someone who really does see the good side of the student and has unconditional, unbiased hopes for the future. This removes any showing off element and allows students to really expect the best.

> 'And the day came when the risk it took to remain tight inside the bud was more painful than the risk it took to blossom'.
>
> *Anais Nin*

Build your confidence

How confident are YOU? What do confident people look like? Sound like? Think Like?

Habit 3:

Have confidence and self-belief

Rate your confidence on this scale:

LOW 1 2 3 4 5 6 7 8 9 10 HIGH

Liking and respecting yourself is the first step to being confident.

Always start by being honest about *you*.

Do you like yourself? Think about it…

Start off by filling in this grid. Be honest!

Then share your points with a friend and ask them if they agree with you.

Add another great thing about you that your friend says is great.

Five great things about me

1. _____
2. _____
3. _____
4. _____
5. _____

Friend says:

_____

_____

Build your confidence

NOW THINK ABOUT WHAT YOU NEED TO WORK ON AND FILL IN THIS GRID.

Ask your friend again and add another.

Three things I need to improve

1. _____

2. _____

3. _____

Friend says:

_____

_____

_____

TASK

Swap sheets with someone who doesn't know you well. Imagine you are like a life coach and student.

Discuss the content of the grids and how you can raise your achievement.

Replay some of these interviews for the whole class to hear.

Get to know your best friend.
YOU!

Build your confidence

Life coach assessment

The other person you have been working with has been acting as a life coach. Rate their skills and discuss what they said that really worked for you and what didn't. Discuss these skills as a class.

Last task – but the most important

Think of someone who loves you (your mum or your carer)?

Imagine that person sitting at your desk now and being in control of your pen.

Write a letter from them to you thanking you for being so great and celebrating your brilliance.

Include their hopes and dreams for your future.

Keep this letter somewhere safe and read it whenever you want to feel confident.

Dear Joe,

I knew the moment you were born that you would be special. As a toddlers you were very beautiful, full of energy and determined ...

Be your own life coach

Habit 3: Have confidence and self-belief

Aim

To help students understand what will build up their self-esteem and how to do it more often.

First thoughts

The starter activity involves students looking at the healthy and unhealthy things we do that can add to or detract from our emotional 'bank balance'.

Then this activity can be shaped into more detail using the line exercise which shows that answers are not black and white.

When the personal bank account deposits are discussed, students can think of specific examples of activity.

Giving life currency scores to activities means placing a value on them and then seeing how the balance looks.

The final statements on this lesson plan can be used for a Community of Enquiry approach in discussion or a written exercise.

(Adapted from an activity in 'Seven Habits of Effective Teenagers' by Sean Covey.)

Be your own life coach

Coach yourself to build up your Personal Bank Account

Habit 3:

Have confidence and self-belief

How you feel about yourself is like your own Personal Bank Account.

How is your Personal Bank Account balance – is it in credit or in debit?

Healthy	Unhealthy
+5 +4 +3 +2 +1 0 −1 −2 −3 −4 −5	
You stand up for yourself	You cave in to peer pressure
You don't worry about being popular	You feel inferior
You enjoy life	You worry too much about what others think
You trust yourself	You act tough to hide insecurities
You have goals	You don't know what you want
You are happy for others to do well	You get jealous of others' success
You can give and receive compliments	You can't give praise
You're okay about making mistakes	You blame yourself or others for getting everything wrong
You eat well and take exercise	You self-destruct with drugs etc

Be your own life coach

TASK

Draw a line out for each of these and show where you stand for each one.

How to coach yourself for a 'richer' life

Make Personal Bank Account Deposits

Keep promises to yourself

Do kind things for people

Be kind to yourself

Use positive self-talk

Be honest with yourself and others

Feed yourself well

Take exercise to release positive endorphins

Nurture your talents

Complete projects

Learn new things

Work out how much each of these deposits is worth in currency.

Make a plan now to show how you are going to do at least 6 of these in the next week.

Start small.

For example:

Deposit Plan

Make a promise to get up early one day this week (€5)

Wash up after a meal at home (€7)

Say to yourself every morning 'I am brilliant' (€10)

Go for a brisk walk for 20 mins (€5)

Finish a piece of homework or coursework – properly (€7)

Total €34 deposit

Be your own life coach

How to coach yourself for a 'poorer' life

Make Personal Bank Account Withdrawals

Break personal promises

Spend time alone

Tell yourself you are rubbish

Be dishonest

Wear yourself out by staying up late

Neglect your talents

Miss meals or eat badly

Say something nasty or bitchy

Make excuses for not completing schoolwork

List any of these (or others) you have done this week. Give them a score and take that away from your total deposits.

See now how your Personal Bank Account balance stands.

Spend some time every week working out how your Personal Bank Account is balanced. Try to build up some credit so that you can feel a difference.

Keep a diary of how you feel.

'Random acts of kindness make you feel the best you can be'.

'The best cure for being depressed is to do something kind for someone else'.

'What goes around – comes around'.

What does this mean? How can it help you coach yourself to a happy life?

Mind Power

Habit 3: Have confidence and self-belief

Build your confidence and self-belief. (This could last up to three school lessons.)

Resources

Music, cards to write affirmations on.

Aim

By the end of this lesson students will have some strategies and skills to make them feel confident and successful when they need to. The aim of this lesson is to convince students that the way they think about their future and themselves can have a significant impact on what happens to them.

First thoughts

First thoughts are about the ways we try to predict our future.

The students will discuss fortune-tellers, palm readers and the like for a whole lesson, as they may be very interested in the subject. Anecdotal stories of predictions that came

true will be forthcoming too. It is worth mentioning that Scottish thane, Macbeth, who went to see a witch and was told he would be king. He then proceeded to make it come true. An interesting discussion about how we make predictions come true is a good introduction to 'creating your own future'.

The action statement affirmations need discussion and thinking through. Are they possible? Could they make a difference?

Metacognition means standing back from thoughts and feelings and observing their impact, in other words, thinking about thinking.

The next exercise is a guided visualisation using NLP techniques. It is also useful to have a song and a statement ready for the visualisation. During this preparation it may be wise to play some inspirational songs to give them ideas. For example, 'I believe I can fly…' by R. Kelly.

Take at least ten minutes to do the visualisation. Use the relaxation exercises first from Section 1 – Lesson 13. During the visualisation remember that the picture created must be extreme, colourful and very memorable to make it work. The emotional brain doesn't respond to the mediocre.

Review

Link back to the fortune-tellers creating your future picture – now you have done this for yourself and given your unconscious mind some anchors to bring back those positive feelings.

Extension and further ideas

Try this at home and try using other feelings such as:
'Remember a time when you were very confident, calm and in control …'.
This uses the same strategy creating a different feeling and anchored for use later.

Try it for phobias. Recall the place where the fear is already anchored, for example in the bedroom. Create a scene where there is time and space to admire and feel comfortable with spiders, like this.

'Imagine a time when you loved spiders. You sat looking at a lovely creature climbing slowly up your bedroom wall and felt calm and in control. You were breathing and relaxing and feeling warm and friendly to the spider. You moved slightly closer to see the spider and gently touched it. You felt calm … and so on'.

This technique plants a positive experience in the unconscious mind, programming it for the next time it meets spiders.

This technique can also be used for behaviour problems.

I say …
"Tell me what it would look like if you were happy and hard working in class. What would it feel like inside, what would you see, hear and say etc…. Think of a word to say that will give you this feeling again and say it the next time you think you are about to get into trouble".

> TIP: Affirmations can be put onto cards and placed in the pocket as reminders.

> **If you can think you can or if you think you can't – you're right.**
> *Henry Ford*

Mind Power

Self-belief – you can create your own future

Habit 3:

Have confidence and self-belief

For many thousands of years human beings have been trying to predict their future without success.

Discuss the following ways of predicting your future:

- horoscopes
- clairvoyants
- tarot cards
- ouija boards
- eating marshmallows (see Lesson 17)
- fortune-tellers
- careers questionnaires
- reading tea leaves
- palm reading

With a partner, list the positive and negative points about these options for fortune telling.

However, there is a way to predict your future by planting seeds of positive thoughts that then grow and become reality … or you can plant weeds and create a negative wasteland. Many of the points in this lesson have been mentioned before. Try them – they really work!

Sow the seeds by creating a positive attitude by taking these actions… *now*.

- Set goals – big ambitious ones that you put up on the wall in your bedroom.

- Create positive mental pictures of your life at school and at home and think about them for several minutes each day.

- See mistakes as learning experiences – there is no such thing as failure only feedback.

- Love yourself and your body.

- Be good to others – give out compliments and kindnesses. They will come back to you eventually.

- See yourself as a good learner.

- Use your inner dialogue to say positive things to yourself – don't let *you* put *you* down.

- Praise your own and other people's success.

- Use metacognition (thinking about your thinking) to develop your understanding of how to manage your mind.

If all of this sounds difficult or ridiculous, then it is no more ridiculous than reading a horoscope or looking at tea leaves to predict your future. See your next challenge as practising thinking positive thoughts if you have the habit of thinking negative ones. Get out of the habit of saying 'I can't'. Say 'I can'.

Mind Power

Tools to help

Music – having songs that make you feel happy, confident and inspired can help. For example, 'I'm a Survivor' by Destiny's Child.

Think of 3 songs that make you feel happy … *now*.

_____

_____

_____

Having a statement that inspires you can really make a difference. These are sometimes called affirmations.

Here are some examples.
Add some more.

> I believe I can fly.
> (R. Kelly)
>
> The harder I work the luckier I get.
> (Samuel Goldwyn)
>
> I can do anything if I believe.

TRY THIS …
MAKING MIND MOVIES

Remember a time when you were a great success – maybe in an exam, a sports day, a performance. If you can't think of a time, create one. Make a movie in your mind of that successful time. Get the picture clear and cinema sized in your head. Turn up the colour, the sound and the size of the picture. *Feel* what it felt like to be that great success. See what you could see, hear what you could hear as everyone complimented you. Keep that feeling going for a few moments then anchor that feeling with a song that makes you feel great. Put it onto your success movie with surround sound. Create an affirmation or statement to go with all this positive feeling. Something like 'I can do it' or 'Go for it'. Say it loud in your head and anchor all those feelings with the statement. Add a gesture to support it – a thumbs up or victory sign perhaps. See it, hear it, act it, be it.

You just created your future.

What you have done is create a positive state of mind for being successful. You can get it back whenever you sing the song or say the words or do the gesture because your unconscious mind will remember that state you created.

The more often you do this the better it will work. So practise at home! Remember to make the movie bright, powerful and colourful.

You can then use your anchored gesture, song or affirmation before exams, interviews or any time you wish to be successful.

Persistence and Resilience

| Habit 4: Be persistent and resilient

> Genius is one per cent inspiration, ninety nine percent perspiration.
> *Thomas Edison, Harper's Monthly 1932*

Aim

To experience and practise what it means to be persistent and resilient.

The starter is a discussion on how all learning is about making mistakes and about learning to fail in order to succeed.

The core of the lesson is to develop on the training to be a life coach ideas of the previous lesson.

Review the qualities of a good coach – this can be related to sport.

The drawing in the wrong hand exercise is a challenge that all will find hard, but you could use juggling or playing an instrument instead. The idea is that the students acting as coach learn what to say and do to keep *their own* spirits up and encourage persistence. By encouraging someone else they are learning the self-talk that might be useful for them.

All successful authors, poets, artists and entrepreneurs experience failure and rejection many times before they finally achieve recognition.

> 'The harder I work the luckier I get'.

Persistence and Resilience

Persistence is the most powerful habit of EQ

Habit 4:
Be persistent and resilient

First thoughts

'I get knocked down
But I get up again,
You're never gonna keep me down…'

('Tubthumping' by Chumbawumba)

Being persistent means taking the knock-backs and still trying,
then taking more knock-backs and still trying,
then being knocked back again and trying again and so on.

How do babies learn to walk?   How do toddlers learn to talk?

Being persistent creates resilience. Being resilient means you can survive and prosper.
It gives you power and strength of character.

By training yourself to be persistent you can become resilient and strong.

TASK

In pairs discuss these statements:

- Practise makes perfect.
- Every mistake is a learning experience.
- There is no such thing as failure only feedback.
- In training I visualise success.

What do you need to help you be persistent and keep trying? Support, encouragement, positive attitude, self-belief or motivation? A coach can help you to try, try, and try again.

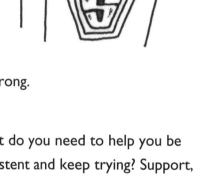

In pairs, one of you draw a dog with your wrong hand. The coach must give the artist advice and encouragement to improve the drawing and make them try 4 more times.

Now swap and see if the new coach has learnt from his own experience of being coached.

Now try the same activity with a blindfolded partner trying to write their full address neatly.

The most important question: How can you be your own life coach to encourage persistence?

Extension

What are the essential qualities for being a good coach?

LESSON 10

Mood Control

Habit 5: Be an optimist

Resources

Mood music.

Aim

By the end of this lesson students will understand how important it is to take control of their own moods.

First thoughts

Monitoring mood is the first task. You do it too and share your experience with the class. You can demonstrate your moods in your posture and facial expression.

Relating body and mind involves understanding the way our bodies are affected by our minds and vice versa.

Make time for a brain booster (Lesson 30).

The group task for drama can show effectively how moods affect other people.

The mood monitor created at the end of the session can be a circle or rectangle with these moods on and some kind of paper clip/arrow that is moveable to show changes. This could be taken home and used every day.

Review

Set your mood monitor. Think of three ways to change a neighbours mood.

Extension

Develop your mood monitor at home.

> People will forget what you say, people will forget what you did, but people will never forget how you made them feel.

Mood Control

Choose to be in a good mood – you can if you want to be...

Habit 5:
Be an optimist –
Take control of
your moods

First thoughts

There are many different types of mood: happiness, sadness, disgust, surprise, anger, fear, frustration, anxiety, hopelessness, fury, guilt, disappointment, loneliness, jealousy, calmness, curiosity, love, excitement, desire, ... to mention just a few!
What mood are you in? Can you help it?
What puts you in a good or a bad mood?

Draw an arrow on this diagram to show where you think you are:

Despair	Depressed	A bit down	OK	Quite good	Good	Very good	Ecstatic

Explain to your neighbour how you know and why you feel like this.

The mood you are in can change the outcome of events. If you can control your moods then you can control your life.

TASK

In pairs: Put your hands in front of your face. When you move them away show a mood on your face which your partner has to guess. Try several different moods.

Your facial expression and your posture are influenced by your mood.

Stand up and show different moods through the way you stand. Show some of these to the rest of the class.

Mood Control

Laugh loudly NOW – Just by physically laughing, endorphins (brain chemicals) are triggered that make you feel good.

When you stand up straight with your head up and a smile on your face it is physiologically impossible to be in a bad mood! TRY IT.

GROUP TASK

It is Monday morning breakfast time.

Act out the typical scene.

Then change the mood of each of the actors to see how it changes the scene.

Your mood has the power to influence others – bad moods are contagious, good moods are infectious and spread happiness.

TASK

Create a mood monitor for your bedroom like the diagram on the first page as a way of monitoring your moods. Using a piece of card and a large paper clip. Assess your mood at the moment and explain why.

Extension

Monitor you mood using this mood monitor over a period of a week and keep a record of how your mood changes and what influences it.

REVIEW

Think of three ways to change your mood or that of your neighbour.

Mood Control

Mood Monitor (example)

Optimism

Habit 5: Be an optimist

Optimism – get the golden glow.

Resources

Coloured paper and pens to make a poster.

First thoughts

What is optimism and where do you stand along the spectrum of Pessimism to Optimism?

One of the most important EQs is optimism – by the end of this lesson you will know how to make yourself into a more optimistic person.

Plan

The first section of the lesson is a class discussion on what optimism is and how it affects us. The story of the optimist and pessimist emphasises that people develop different tendencies but that doesn't mean they have to stay that way. The fact that we can *choose* the way we think needs to be emphasised.

Use this story to demonstrate the point:

Once there was a father of two children, one a pessimist and one an optimist. One Christmas he asked them to draw up a list of all the presents they wanted – anything and everything. He bought the pessimist everything on her list, wrapped the presents up and put them in her bedroom on Christmas Eve. He bought the optimist a lorry load of manure and put that at the end of her bed on the night before Christmas.

On Christmas morning he was astonished to hear his pessimistic child crying and his optimistic child whooping in delight.

'What's wrong? You got all these lovely presents…' he said to the pessimist.

'I have all these lovely presents and all my friends are going to hate me and be jealous'. 'And…and…' sobbed the pessimist, 'how am I ever going to have time to play with all these lovely things…?'

Sighing, the father went to his second child who was laughing and jumping about in glee.

'What did you get for Christmas that has made you so happy?'

'I GOT A LOAD OF MANURE…AND IT'S ALL AT THE END OF MY BED …WHOOPEEE…' she shrieked.

'Why on earth does that make you so happy?' he asked.

'Well I figure, with that much manure around there must be a pony in there somewhere... '

> *This story prompts the question: Can you change the way you think?*

Can you turn any situation around by thinking about it differently?

The statements in the next section are worth saying around the class so that students can hear how negative some language is – and how often they use that negative language.

Reframing a situation is a very useful exercise. Students can think of some more situations to reframe.

The discussion on how some people turn good luck into bad and vice versa could be conducted in groups with a feedback session.

Time for a brain booster session (Lesson 30).

Students should make a big list of all the positive things in their life on large paper to pin up on the bedroom wall and look at when they feel down.

Review

Say something optimistic to your friend before you leave the lesson – leave the room smiling and smile at three people you don't know at break.

Optimism

OPTIMISM – get the golden glow

Habit 5:
Be an optimist

Where are you?

Low   1   2   3   4   5   6   7   8   9   10   High

Optimism is infectious. Make sure you spread happiness – not misery!

It's all about seeing the positive side of a situation – trying to find the silver lining in every cloud. Making this a habit.

Have you got it?
If you have you will be more successful in life – and that's a fact!

How do you feel?

- If your best friend gets a new computer and you still have an ancient machine

  Do you feel jealous and angry?
  OR
  Do you look forward to having a go?

- You get a low score in a test you had revised for because you didn't answer the questions properly

  Do you moan and decide never to work hard again?
  OR
  Do you pester your teacher to find out just what you did wrong because you are determined your work will pay off next time?

What are you more likely to say or think?

Saying stuff creates a way of thinking.

This is really boring	This is interesting
I can't do this	My mates are great
No one likes me	It's a lovely day
It's raining again	You look good today
That's typical	I'm just born lucky
Just my luck	Teachers like me
I hate maths	I'll eat anything!
Teachers hate me	Learning stuff is great
Everyone picks on me	I'm brilliant
I'm not eating that!	I enjoyed that lesson
School is a waste of time	I'm really trying to do this

Optimism

TASK

a) Think of some more sayings for each column. It might sound cool to be negative about everything – especially school – but if you are negative, **you will programme your brain to switch off. If you are positive, you will become a great learner.**

b) Try saying the statements on the right in lots of different ways – **you will find yourself feeling good just by saying it.**

Now take each statement on the left and write or say a positive response to turn it round. You could add: BUT….

Top tips to get the golden glow of optimism

Discuss these and copy them into your planner

- SMILE – research shows that people who smile a lot are more successful in life. Try it *now*.

- Compliment others – do it every day. Make people feel better after they have come into contact with you.

- Look in the mirror every morning and tell yourself you are brilliant, beautiful and have a great sense of humour!!!

- Whenever you have a negative thought, *reframe* it and see the silver lining – there is always one there – by saying …

- *It could be much worse.*

- *I can learn something from this.*

- *It will make me stronger as I learn strategies to cope and my brain makes new connections.*

- *If it doesn't kill me it makes me stronger!!*

CHALLENGE

Create a Recipe for Optimism Cake. Include the important ingredients that make people feel positive and how to mix them up. Draw a picture of the cake to show what it might look life.

Optimism Cake

Ingredients   Amounts

TASK – Sparkling story.

Write a story of a time when you sparkled – when you were at your very best and were amazing. Exaggerate it and write it in the present tense.

For example: 'It's a wonderful spring day, I wake up, yawn and glance in the mirror. I look absolutely gorgeous, handsome, natural and ready for a brilliant day …'

> *Now list all the good things in your life and pin this on your bedroom wall.*

LESSON 12

Taking care of mind and body

Habit 6: Take care of yourself – body and brain

Manage your Mind and Body.

Aims

To help students understand how to manage their mind and body to be healthy and fit for learning.

Background

This section revisits some previous ideas within the course, but adds important information demonstrating the important links between physical and mental well-being. The medical and educational case for healthy eating are well made and accepted.

First thoughts

The starter activity is an audit of food eaten. This can be completed on the sheet or in the book. Then the foods can be discussed in some depth.

Task

Creating a menu can be done in pairs and presented on nice menu cards as in a hotel.

After the discussion on sleep, exercise and fun, the menu idea could be extended to become a publicity campaign leaflet with advice on health and fitness for teenagers.

"Use it or lose it", gives students a chance to consider how their lifestyle affects their learning.

Review

Discuss with a neighbour how you are going to take at least one action to make yourself healthier.

Extension

Several extension activities are suggested in the spirit of encouraging independent learning. Link with what students know about diet from science lessons.

On the Internet research health and fitness for teenagers.

teacher's notes

Section 1 • The Habits of Emotional Intelligence

Taking care of mind and body

Manage your mind and body

Habit 6: Take care of yourself – body and brain

First thoughts

Feed your body and feed your brain.

What you put inside your body really does affect your brain.

Write down everything you eat in a normal school day.

YOU ARE WHAT YOU EAT

Check the list below to see if you have eaten foods that are good for your body and your brain...or not?

Get results with:

Carbohydrates such as wholemeal bread, bagels, muffins

Fruit – you need that vitamin C

Vegetables – especially green ones

Lean meat, or cereals, nuts and beans if you are a veggie

Bananas – good for stamina

Cereals – especially oats

Pasta and rice

Salad

Fish

WATER – essential for learning – drink at least 8 glasses a day.

Chocolate – some say it is good for you!

Avoid:

Sugar and any sugary foods like sweets

Coffee in large amounts

Alcohol (in any amount)

Fizzy drinks – especially colas

Artificial flavourings – lots of 'e' numbers

Too many fatty foods such as chips and burgers

Chocolate – some say it is bad for you!

Cigarettes – they contain nicotine which is a powerful, addictive drug

Cannabis can create paranoia and depression, and it is illegal!

'It's easy to give up smoking – I've done it a hundred times' Mark Twain

Taking care of mind and body

TASK

Challenge – can you turn the 'Get Results' list into an appetising menu for your friends?

Create a brain friendly menu for the day for a typical teenager from the list of healthy foods.

WORK HARD – PLAY HARD ...and sleep well... Food affects your mood.

You need to keep your body fit and healthy with exercise.

Do your brain boosters (Lesson 30) every day to wake up your brain.

Try to exercise at least three times a week for 20 minutes each time by:

- cycling
- dancing
- walking,
- swimming
- jogging
- aerobics (get a DVD)
- team sports

Sleep is crucial too. Make sure you get 8 hours. Use the relaxation exercise in Lesson 13 if you need help getting to sleep. If you do lie in bed awake then use the time to think happy positive thoughts about yourself and to plan your next steps.

Have fun, enjoy yourself – do something every day that you enjoy.

Make a list of the things you enjoy doing.

Do they include any of the things that are good for you – if not add some.

Have fun, enjoy yourself – do something every day that you enjoy.

Taking care of mind and body

Use it or lose it

Keeping healthy means feeding your brain too.

When you learn new stuff your brain grows more connections and keeps healthy. If you coast through your school years you could go backwards. Remember you can develop your brain power through hobbies, part-time jobs, learning at home, watching TV, gardening and any extra curricular activities as well as school learning.

What have you learnt this week?

Write a list of all your learning experiences in the past week.

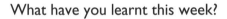

Extension

● Keep a learning diary

● Read a quality newspaper

● Paint a picture

● Learn to play an instrument

● Travel!

LESSON 13

Stress Management

Habit 6: Take care of yourself – body and brain

Manage your mind and manage your stress.

Resources

First thoughts are about the connotations of stress and how students perceive it.

By the end of this lesson you will understand how to control stress more effectively.

First thoughts

The first part of the lesson focuses on the positive side of stress to counteract preconceptions.

Time for some brain boosters (Lesson 30).

Plan the discussion about the positive side of stress helps students appreciate that adrenaline can work for us, not just against us.

The strategies for coping with stress can be shared with the class when completed, as can the internal dialogue ideas in the next task.

The relaxation exercise should take about 8 minutes, it should not be rushed. For some students this will be an ideal technique to use again during exams.

TIP

When they are relaxed give them an anchor – a word or phrase – that means they can switch on this feeling again. It could be just: *relax* or *now I feel great*.

Making a stress buster business card is something that can be taken away and kept, to remind students of how to combat stress.

Review

Share three ways to deal with stress with a neighbour.

Extension

Design a leaflet or create a role-play that could be performed in assembly.

Practise the relaxation exercises in bed to help you get to sleep.

Section 1 • The Habits of Emotional Intelligence

teacher's notes

Stress Management

Manage your mind and your stress

Habit 6: Take care of yourself – body and brain

First thoughts

What is stress?

Is it good or bad?

Do we need it?

What is it for?

Life without any stress would be quite dull – adrenalin makes life exciting.

List what happens to your mind and body when you experience stress.

We all experience different kinds of stress in different situations, but some people are much better at handling it than others.

TASK

Discuss three situations you find stressful with your partner, then share them with the class.

1. _____

2. _____

3. _____

Animals need the adrenaline that stress gives to run away from predators.

List 5 reasons why we need stress:

1. _____

2. _____

3. _____

4. _____

5. _____

Coping with stress and making it into a positive force is important in life.

'Stress does my head in'

… but it doesn't have to… When you feel threatened your unconscious mind sends signals to your body to run or react. Your heart beats faster and your blood rushes to your brain. You become more powerful – so use it positively. It can help you perform better!

TOP TIP: Eat well, sleep well and exercise to decrease excess stress.

Stress Management

Here are five strategies for coping with stress … **add five more**.

1. Go for a walk in the fresh air

2. Think calm relaxing thoughts

3. Talk to a friend

4. Play some good music

5. Use relaxation techniques

6. _____

7. _____

8. _____

9. _____

10. _____

INTERNAL DIALOGUE

Talking to yourself inside your head is very useful when coping with stress.

Write down 3 things you could say to yourself when stressed that will help.

1._____

2._____

3._____

It's not what happens to you but it's the way you deal with it that matters.

Relaxation exercises (put some relaxing music on for this).

Try this… Now!

Breathe deeply in and out 5 times.
As you breathe out imagine all the stress and aggro wafting out into space and leaving your body.

Now screw up your fists really tight, tighter, then relax, let your hands lay gently on your lap.

Now feel the relaxation travel down through your legs and to the floor. Imagine all your stress and tension pouring out into the floor and flowing away into the earth's crust. As you do this your body will feel soft and peaceful.

Roll your head around slowly and breathe softly as you roll your shoulders, one at a time.
Close your eyes and imagine you are lying on a soft sandy beach with the sun gently shining and the sound of waves lapping gently onto the shore.

As you stretch and come back to reality you feel ready to cope with anything in a calm and positive way.

Stress Management

TASK

Make a stress-buster card.

Create a small business card. On it put a stress buster slogan and a relaxing logo such as a bird or an angel, the title of a song that makes you feel good and a smiley cartoon self portrait.

Keep this in your wallet or purse and look at it when you feel stressed.

Extension work

Design a leaflet for teenagers on how to cope with stress.

OR

Role-play a scene where a teenager goes to a stress counsellor.

Swap these ideas with a neighbour and see if they have similar ideas.

TASK

In groups of 3 or 4 try this role-play.

A student is not completing homework for a variety of reasons. The parents have come to visit the teacher to get some help and advice on how to improve the situation. Role-play the scene. You are the teacher. You must use the information you have learned in this and other lessons to give good advice to the parents and student. Each person should have a turn as the teacher.

LESSON 14

Thinking skills

Habit 6: Take care of yourself – body and brain

Build your brain power.

Resources

Large paper and pens for group work.

Aim

By the end of this lesson students will have practised creative and analytical thinking skills.

Starter

Employers want students who can think creatively. It may be worth some class discussion time on why that is.

Plan

Consider the problems. Choose only *one* problem to solve in groups of four.

Follow instructions to think through solutions.

Review

What is the difference between creative and analytical thinking?

Extension and follow on

Follow up next lesson with other problems, following the same structure of thinking.

Thinking skills

Build your brain power

Famous, successful people like Albert Einstein, Bill Gates and Richard Branson used their creative and analytical powers to become rich and famous. It is important to have new ideas but it is just as important to be able to organise the ideas and test them out. You too can develop these skills.

Habit 6: Take care of yourself – body and brain

Choose one of these real problems to solve:

- Too many cars in the country.
- Too many people in the world.
- Too little food to feed the world.
- Too little money to run your school.

You can work in pairs or groups:

Be a creative thinker

Define the problem.

Brainstorm information and organise key words into a learning map.

Generate lots of ideas, as wild and whacky as you like. Write them down.

Mix the ideas up together and come up with up to five different solutions to the problem.

Then

Be an analytical thinker

Imagine you are a detective – switch off your emotional brain and be practical and unbiased as you do the following:

Examine each idea – test it out with a SWOT test

Strengths

Weaknesses

Opportunities

Threats

Creative thinkers take risks *and* challenge their mind to think outside of the box.

Analytical thinkers need to be cool, calm and objective, with great attention to detail. Asking the right questions is an important skill.

On the basis of this analysis throw out all but two of the ideas.

Now work out the plus, minus and interesting bits – PMI – for each remaining idea (this method was developed by Edward De Bono).

PLUS   MINUS   INTERESTING BITS

Choose an idea and using the above methods, make a proposal to sell it to people explaining why it is the best option.

Present your ideas to the class.

LESSON 15

Asking the right questions

Habit 6: Take care of yourself – body and brain

Resources

Lined paper/whiteboards.

Asking the right questions is an essential competence for the 21st century.
By the end of this lesson students will understand how important questioning is and how to form good questions.

Plan

This lesson works well using whiteboards and timing the exercises to create challenge.

Follow the lesson plan as instructed on the sheet. Students have to create questions on topics.

The 8Way Thinking Tool will encourage thinking around a topic.

Review

A good question:

- It is open, not closed.
- It makes you think.
- It demands certain interesting information.
- It uses clear words and punctuation.

Assessment opportunity

Get students to rate their own questions out of 10 to make them aware what makes a good question.

Extension

Students can look at exam questions and plan answers. Then they can work backwards by looking at exam answers and guessing the questions. This is excellent preparation for exams.

> **Asking questions is the secret to success.**

teacher's notes

Asking the right questions

Build your brain power

Habit 6:
Take care of yourself – body and brain

You learn more from asking questions than from answering them.
To ask questions you need to be creative in your thinking.
You need to work back to front.

If these are the answers think of three possible questions for each statement:

Yes, we have no bananas.

It's raining men.

I haven't stopped dancing yet.

Why do birds suddenly appear?
(Can a question produce another question?)

Think of 3 more answers and get your partner to think of the questions.
Share the best examples with the class.

A good question pushes back the boundaries of knowledge and shows you are engaging your brain with learning.

Work with a partner to create two or three questions on each of these topics using the 8Way Thinking Tool on the following page.

- *Popular music*
- *The internet*
- *Skateboarding*
- *The moon*

Can you answer any of your questions? Can anyone else? How could you tell if they were useful questions?

Write down here the definition of a useful question for learning.

Being good at asking questions is important in many professions.

Imagine you or your partner is a suspect in a case of burglary in your home area.

Your partner is to interrogate you. Create ten crucial questions to ask about the event that will move the case forward. Try them out.

Asking the right questions

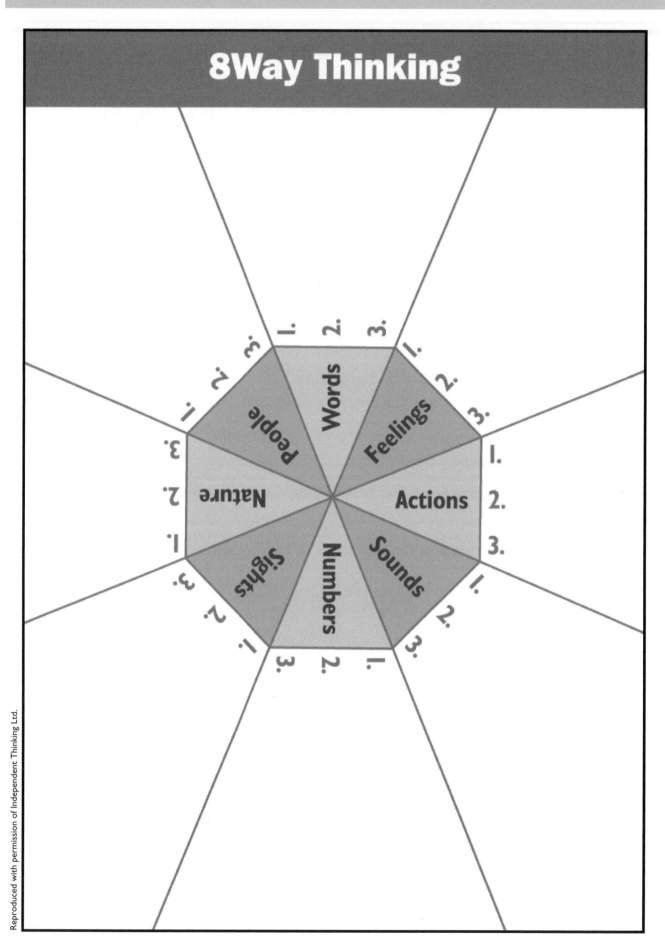

8Way Thinking

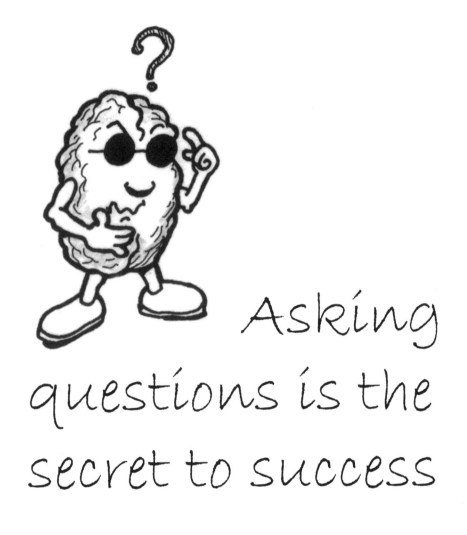

Asking questions is the secret to success

Mastering your memory

Habit 6: Take care of yourself – body and brain

Training your brain to remember.

Aim

To learn some techniques which will train the memory to remember important information.

Resources

Teachers can use a covered tray of items to test short-term memory recall.

Starter

This explores the things that are retained in the memory.

The following exercises provide practice in using the emotional brain to remember things by making them emotional and memorable.

Once students have rehearsed the methods they can make up some of their own tips and tricks.

The best extension of this task is to use the techniques to revise for tests that are part of the curriculum. You can spend another whole lesson to do this.

Mastering your memory

Training your brain to remember

Habit 6: Take care of yourself – body and brain

At least 70% of what you learn today may be forgotten by tomorrow unless you make a special effort to remember it. However, your memory can be amazing. Jot down now everything that is in your bedroom. Now write down every phone number that you know. Remember some adverts from the TV – how many can you think of?

Yes, your memory is good but what can you remember about what you have learnt in lessons this week?

Your memory works by making associations – the greater and stronger the links between things the better you will be able to remember.

Try this:

Learn these pairs of nouns

car   ring
house   book
sky   rabbit
hat   sausage
computer   flower

How did you learn them? – Did you make mental pictures or use other words to link them together to make sentences. Research shows the best way to remember is to make whacky mental images.
(For example, a car driving through a massive ring.)

Rhyming is a powerful way to help you remember. Here is a shopping list to memorise:

ice cream
carrots
potatoes
baked beans
soap
chocolate
biscuits
bread
orange juice
pork chops

Take a minute to memorise the list then see how many you can recall.

Now create a whacky rhyme for each word and a mad image to go with it.

How many can you remember now?

TIP: Learning names is easy if you use alliteration. For example, Gentle Joe or Saucy Sarah, Perfect Paul, Mad Matthew.

Mastering your memory

Use mnemonics to help your memory

This means using letters to make up phrases that help you remember.

For example:

This formula for trigonometry you need for Key Stage 3 Maths

Sine = Opposite/Hypoteneuse

Cosine = Adjacent/Hypoteneuse

Tangent = Opposite/Adjacent

The first letters say SOHCAHTOA – which is much easier to remember.

For example:

You may find spelling 'necessary' is hard to remember.

But Never Eat Cakes Eat Salad, Sandwiches And Remain Young is easier to remember.

What does 'ROYGBIV' stand for?

The Learner's Toolkit © Jackie Beere and Crown House Publishing Ltd

Mastering your memory

Make up some of your own mnemonics.

> **TIP:** Using mental pictures, associations, mnemonics and rhyming techniques are powerful aids to your memory. Advertisers know this – How well can any of you remember any radio advertising slogans? Why did you learn them? Did you need to?

Try

definitely

chaos

Which words do you get wrong?

What are the different maths or science formulae?

$$s = \frac{d}{t} \qquad F = ma$$

REVIEW is an essential part of learning and memory. If you top up your learning on a regular basis you will find it stays with you.

Review NOW all the tips you have learnt this lesson about how to improve your memory.

Train your brain to wait

Habit 7: Practise self-discipline and willpower

How to develop your willpower.

Aim

By the end of this lesson students will know how important it is to have the willpower to wait for things they really want.

First thoughts

Are you a grinder or a grabber?
A grinder is someone who grinds away at things and works tirelessly; a grabber is a person who grabs what they can get quickly and without too much effort, living in the moment.

Plan

The story is simplified from the Daniel Goleman book based on a real piece of research conducted in America.

Students really enjoy the story and understand the implications.

Discussions about when they need to wait or have willpower are worthwhile to give ideas for the role play.

Tip

Children have to create the connections for deferred gratification, so if they never have their needs frustrated at home they may find it very hard to tolerate frustration. The important thing for them to realise is that it is good for them!

Review

How can lack of willpower destroy your life?

Extension

Teach this lesson to parents!

Train your brain to wait

Train your brain to wait – the rewards will be amazing

Habit 7:

Practise self-discipline and willpower

Have you got willpower?

Are you a 'grinder' or a 'grabber'? Do you 'grab' at what you want immediately or 'grind' away working at something until you get it right?

The Marshmallow Story
(adapted from D. Goleman, 1997)

Once upon a time in America there was a group of five-year-old children who all loved to eat marshmallows. These children were all clever and keen to work hard at school. They all had the same IQ and a similar family background. One day a researcher decided to conduct an experiment to find out who from this group of children would be most successful later in life. He brought a huge plate of marshmallows into the room where the children were playing and then gave them some brief instructions:

'You can have one marshmallow now but if you wait for about ten minutes while I pop out for a cup of coffee, you can have two marshmallows when I get back. You choose, eat now or wait until later for more.'

Some children gobbled up the marshmallow straight away but others waited for the researcher to return. Those that waited used strategies to distract themselves from temptation. Some sang songs to themselves to keep their mind occupied and others ran around the room or stood facing the wall. When the researcher returned they enjoyed two marshmallows, whilst the others looked on enviously.

Ten years later, when the children were 15 years old, there was a huge difference between the children who waited and those that didn't.

What do you think it was?

Those that had waited were two grades higher in their SATS scores. They were happier and coping better with the demands of school life.

Ten years later when the children were 25 years old there were even more differences between the 'grinders' and the 'grabbers'.

Train your brain to wait

What do you think they were?

Those who had waited were in more successful jobs, careers and relationships. The children who couldn't wait were much more involved with drugs and alcohol and were more likely to have been already married and divorced.

> **Could anything have changed the outcome?**

> **What can you learn from this story?**

TASK

Finish the list below of typical habits of 'grinders' and 'grabbers'.

Create 6 strategies for developing your willpower.

For example:
Going to the gym or training with a sports team.
Open a savings account.

Grinders	**Grabbers**
Take time to do it right	*Rush through a task*
Prepared to save up	*Spend any money immediately*

People will forget what you said
People will forget what you did
But people will never forget
The way you made them feel

Having courage to think in other ways – Thinking hats

Habit 8: Have courage

Resources

Paper for creating hats, scissors, coloured pencils or pens or coloured paper – white, red, black, yellow, green and blue.

Aim

By the end of this lesson you will be able to identify six different ways of thinking and find out how useful it can be to use them.

First thoughts

Why does it take courage to think in different ways?

Plan

Explain the definition of the thinking hats and ask students to draw them on paper, using the colours and appropriate, different designs. These can be used to identify the student's usual approach to thinking.

The activity involving planning the holiday will take some time (about 15 minutes) as students get used to identifying their comments with the thinking hats on.

The whole group exercise in which they put on a certain colour hat is a useful way to understand how ideas can be viewed from different angles.

Review

Class discussion on the week ahead of them. For each comment made assess which thinking hat is on.

Extension

Plan for your next exams/tests using the thinking hats. Have a statement for each hat about the exam. Note which ones you would normally say. Put the yellow thinking hat on more often for a positive outcome.
Reference to Edward De Bono for this model.

> 'Imagination is everything. It is the preview of life's coming attractions'.
> *Albert Einstein*

Having courage to think in other ways

Thinking hats

Edward De Bono suggests that we need six different types of thinking hat to wear in order to see issues in different ways.

Design a different shaped hat for each colour.	
White hat	Neutral and objective. White hat cares about facts and figures.
Red Hat	Angry and emotional.
Black Hat	Serious and sensible, cautious and careful.
Yellow hat	Sunny and positive, an optimistic way of thinking.
Green hat	New ideas, creativity and growth.
Blue hat	Cool and above everything like the sky. Blue takes control and organises the other hats.

Think about the hats. Which hat do you wear most often, least often – never??

Using these coloured hats for thinking means we can consciously make our thinking work in certain ways.

In a group you are planning the holiday of your dreams. Use a piece of sugar paper to make your plans and use the thinking hats to see it from all directions.

When each person speaks they must pick a hat up to show what sort of thinking their comments represent. You must use the different hats as often as possible.

Report back to the rest of the group how the thinking hats affected your planning.

Now all put on the black hat and say something about the holiday you have planned.

Now all put on the yellow hat and say something about the holiday you have planned.

Cut out the hats you have drawn and use them for the next exercise.

Pick up the correct hat for each of these comments about school.

- I hate school because no one likes me.
- Let's see what everyone thinks.
- The exam results for this school are quite impressive.
- Isn't it time we had mixed age groups for lessons.
- School days are the best time of your life.
- Take care that you learn enough at school because you won't have another chance.

Grow your confidence and courage

Habit 8: Have courage

For the starter consider what we mean by courage and whether students consider they have this quality.

First thoughts

Students consider scary activities. This will provide intresting contrasts of opinion. Conclude that fear *is* a state of mind.

Aim

To make students consider ways they can have more courage to take risks.

The main part of the lesson is to copy out two circles or squares that show where their comfort zone is and why some things are scary.

The discussion on phobias is an opportunity to describe the physical features of fear in an open and honest way.

Straying out of the comfort zone in an imaginary way is the first step towards facing up to fears in real life.

Public speaking is one of the most feared activities in life, so getting students to tackle this one in the plenary could be a challenge.

If you can dream it, you can do it.

Grow your confidence and courage

Open to new ideas – making every mistake a learning experience

Habit 8:

Have courage

> Whatever you can do
> Or dream you can,
> begin it.
> Boldness has genius,
> Power and magic in it.
> *Goethe*

First thoughts

Which of these would you do?

	Would do	Might do	Never do
Parachuting			
Travel by train alone			
Pick up a spider			
Complain about a product in a shop or café			
Backpack to Australia			
Go to a party alone			
Speak up against a group if you disagree			
Audition for 'The X Factor'			

Grow your confidence and courage

Take your 'never do' list and write bubbles like the one below that show what you think.

I'm scared of...
I don't like it.
It's not my thing.

Grow your confidence and courage

Now think of five more scary things that you would find difficult to do and discuss what would make you do them.

Why should you challenge yourself to do things that are hard and different?

START
Do something that challenges you

Make mistakes, get it wrong and then put it right

You feel more confident about trying something new

Your brain learns to adapt and grow

Confidence Boot Camp

Create a weekend boot camp programme to help build up courage and an open-minded approach. The camp should have all sorts of challenges for teenagers – physical, emotional and intellectual. List them.

Now design some publicity material to convince teenagers to come on the course.

Courage – be brave, take risks and push yourself out of your comfort zone

Habit 8: Have courage

This lesson is to encourage risk-taking behaviour that develops confidence and courage. The questions at the start investigate the components of courage and reflect on students own perceptions of their own courage.

First thoughts

Think of some questions about personal courage.

Activity

Drawing a circle and putting all the things that they feel comfortable with inside will be very enlightening. Where does school sit? What about flying?

The discussion on phobias will be interesting and may uncover some personal stories that will need following up.

'There is no such thing as failure – only feedback'.

No one can persuade another to change. Each of us guards a gate of change that can only be opened from the inside. We cannot open the gate of another, either by argument or by emotional appeal.
Marilyn Ferguson

teacher's notes

Courage – be brave

Take risks and push yourself out of your comfort zone

Habit 8:
Have courage

Start thinking…

What is the bravest thing you have ever done?

What have you done that has taken some courage?

What would you do if the wing of the plane you're in caught fire?

What would you do if someone called for help from behind a wall?

None of us knows how brave we would be in an emergency situation, but in the long run it is more important to be brave in your own life and constantly push yourself out of your comfort zone.

This means being open to new ideas and activities.

Draw a circle (see next page) and put all the things you normally do inside it.

Put things you find uncomfortable outside the circle.

Courage – be brave

What are you scared of?

Fantasised **E**xperiences **A**ppearing **R**eal

The FEAR factor

> What presses your panic buttons?
>
> What happens to your body?
>
> What is claustrophobia?
>
> Discuss in a group what other phobias you know?
>
> Why do people get phobias?
>
> How can they overcome them?

How to have courage

Choose something from the outside of your circle that you would like to do.

Now take control of your thinking and self-talk.

Give yourself motivation – think of reasons why you want to do it.

Imagine yourself doing it – and loving it.

Visualise how you will feel when you have done it.

> **The more you push yourself out of your comfort zone the stronger and braver you will become.**

Do This Challenge
(This will take courage!)

Stand up and explain to the class what courageous thing you would like to do and why. Describe doing it in the present tense for a couple of sentences.

Courage – be brave

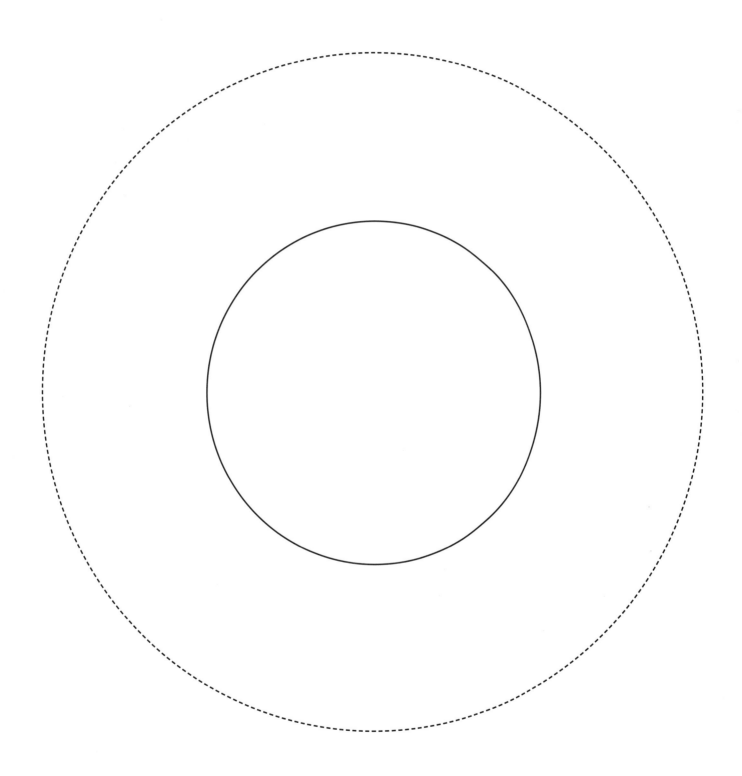

Empathy – put yourself in other's shoes

Habit 9: Co-operate and communicate

The starter is to consider how easy it is to get on with friends. However, it is more demanding but just as important to get on with others. Becoming adaptable and flexible as a communicator is an important competence.

Resources

Card and scissors to make empathy glasses. If time is short, make the glasses in advance and give them out.

Aim

The aim is to use a practical device – the empathy glasses – to be able to see situations in a different perspective.

By the end of this lesson students will know how important and difficult it is to try to see things from other people's viewpoint.

Class discussion on empathy.

Empathy glasses can become a way to understand how to see things from another's viewpoint.

Tip

Students love to make the glasses but they take a long time and distract them from the purpose of the lesson.

Talking for one minute on each of the statements with and without empathy glasses works well.

The discussion how to improve empathy could well be enhanced by reference to the society without empathy, what would it be like and so on.

Some of the role-plays can be shown to others.

The last task is important for transference of skills and ideas into the main curriculum.

Review

So what was empathy again?

> **The meaning of your communication is the response you get.**

Empathy

Put yourself in other's shoes

Habit 9:

Co-operate and communicate

Empathy is an important part of EQ.

Getting on with others is interpersonal intelligence.

How good are you at working with others?

Having empathy will create good relationships.

How well do you get on with: 10/10 is high

Your friends (easy)	/10
Your sisters and brothers (harder)	/10
Your mum and dad/carers (can be hard)	/10
Your teachers (very hard)	/10
Your neighbours (harder still)	/10
People you don't know yet (hardest)	/10

If you are a good communicator you will get on well with others – including people you don't know. In life there will be many occasions when you need to communicate with people you don't know. Most people who are successful know how to put themselves in other people's shoes. They are good listeners and can make themselves understood.

Make a pair of empathy glasses from card and put them on when you need to make a conscious decision to see another person's viewpoint.

In pairs, choose one of these statements and give your opinion about it in one minute:

- Students should be paid to go to school.
- Bullies should be forgiven.
- Parents should be allowed to smack their children.
- There should be no homework for children.
- Drugs should be legalised.

Now argue the opposite view to each other with your empathy glasses on. Score your empathy factor for each other out of ten.

Role-plays are a good way of improving communication and empathy.

Neighbourhood nightmare. Play roles of an old pensioner, young vandals, the village policeman, the school caretaker and so on. Each gives a statement about trouble that has been going on in the village. Swap roles.

Communicate and co-operate for success

Habit 9: Co-operate and communicate

This lesson is about being good at teamwork and getting on with others in the group.

The starter investigates altruism.

The main task is about thinking of ways to compliment others and make them happy. It seems obvious but students benefit from considering explicitly what it takes to gain the crucial skills of creating rapport.

If there is time, the class can form teams, choose a charity and plan a campaign to raise money. One of the aims would be for all the members of the group to contribute and feel supported by everyone else in the group. Each member could vote on the other member's performance as a team member.

teacher's notes

Communicate and co-operate for success

First thoughts

There is nothing better than working in a team and sharing success, but sometimes it feels more like life is a competition and everyone else is out to get you.

Being a good team player is one of the main skills employers are looking for. Sometimes that means putting your own needs or views into the background for the good of others. It also means bringing out the best in others. Think of two examples where you have put someone else's needs before your own.

Helping others succeed is a sure way of raising your self-esteem. Every good deed you do will come back to you again and again, though not always straightaway. Be generous, you will not regret it in the long run.

> **Habit 9:**
>
> Co-operate and communicate
>
>

TASK

Learn to compliment others – and mean it.

Write down 6 compliments about members of your class. (Not just your friends!)

1. _____

2. _____

3. _____

4. _____

5. _____

6. _____

Take it in turns to volunteer to deliver the compliments and mean them. It is just as important to accept the compliments from others by making eye contact, smiling and saying thank you.

Communicate and co-operate for success

TASK

In a group: Think of 6 ways of helping someone else succeed or be happy.
Present your ideas to the class.

1. _____

2. _____

3. _____

4. _____

5. _____

6. _____

Rapport is a French term which means getting on together.
If you can get rapport it makes people like you from the first meeting.

Communicate and co-operate for success

BODY LANGUAGE matters to get RAPPORT

Practise with a partner you don't know. Ask them 3 questions about themselves.

Keep eye contact.

Mirror their position.

Smile and nod.

Keep your shoulders back, and head up.

Listen carefully to what they say and feedback to show you understand.

TOP TIPS: Work with as many different people every day as you can – don't just work with your friends.

Be proactive in making new friends. Don't wait for people to talk to you.

Keep your body language open, have good eye contact and always smile.

Ask questions with interest and listen closely to the answers.

Extension work

Investigate a charity and how you could raise funds by creating a mini campaign.

LESSON 23

Prioritise and plan

Habit 10: Prioritise and plan

By the end of this lesson students will have some strategies for becoming well organised with your work in school and at home.

First thoughts

Some self reflection or the ability and inclination to plan.

Ensure that the checklists can be done as an audit of organisational skills and plan an opportunity to talk through why they are important.

From these lists students could choose the more important points for them and copy them into their books or planners.

The learning environment task can include a sketch to clarify thinking.

Finally, the role-play gives students a chance to use the information learned to give advice to others.

Review

Show presentations and discuss.
Link this lesson into using school planners or diaries.

> **Do the worst first.**

Section 1 • The Habits of Emotional Intelligence

Prioritise and plan

Get organised for learning – BE PROACTIVE

Don't wait for your teacher or your mum/carer to organise you.
When you teach yourself to be proactive, organising yourself is easy!

Habit 10:

Prioritise and plan

Last week – did you:

Plan your week?

Prioritise what you had to do?

Meet all your deadlines?

Arrange any social activities?

Set any goals or targets?

Set any deadlines?

Give in all homework?

Spend time relaxing?

If you answered **No** to lots of these questions
you may need to get more organised.

This list will help you with school, work and life planning. Tick any you do now:

☐ Keep a list of things to do.

☐ Chunk your learning – do 20 minute sessions – use brain boosters in between. See Lesson 30.

☐ Get immediate feedback – ask parents or teachers to comment.

☐ Reward yourself.

☐ Have regular throwing out sessions when you sort out your bag or desk.

☐ Use a planner or diary – this is crucial. Do you write notes to yourself in it and tick things off as you do them.

☐ Keep a notebook to jot down important things.

☐ Vary your learning styles – remember read it, do it, say it, hear it.

☐ Test yourself on what you have learned.

Prioritise and plan

Are you a procrastinator?

Procrastinators put things off until the last minute and seldom get them done on time, or well.

Procastinators can get into a spiral of decline which can end in low self-esteem. Think now of some affirmations you can say when you feel tempted to procrastinate.

Write down 10 things you **have** to do this week and 10 things you **want** to do (be reasonable!)

What I **have** to do this week	What I **want** to do
1.	1.
2.	2.
3.	3.
4.	4.
5.	5.
6.	6.
7.	7.
8.	8.
9.	9.
10.	10.

Now pick the most important 5 from each list and number them one to five with one being the most important.

1.	1.
2.	2.
3.	3.
4.	4.
5.	5.

Prioritise and plan

The Learning Environment

The place you work in as well as the way you work can make a big difference. Create the learning environment that suits you:

Write a paragraph describing your favourite learning environment. Where is it? Time of day? Any music? Food for grazing? Working with friends? What clothes? Using books or the Internet?

My favourite learing environment

LESSON 24

Review the habits of EQ

Review the habits of EQ (Assessment)

Habits for Success – rate yourself.

This is an opportunity to revisit the habits and assess progress and achievement.
This involves reading through with the students all the habits and the behaviours involved with these habits. The students then assess themselves against the habits. One is low, five is high.

They then pick out their 3 lowest scores and copy out the behaviours and top tips and sayings for those 3 habits. These will then form their targets to be reviewed later in the term.

Extension

Those who finish can role-play the life coach interview that talks through the 3 targets and makes suggestions how to move forward.

teacher's notes

Review the habits of EQ

Habits for success

Get the habit	Rating 1–5	How	Top tips and sayings
Take responsibility for yourself		No excuses, be pro-active, take responsibility for your life and everything that happens in it.	*If it's to be, it's up to me.*
Create goals for life		Have a goal and set targets to get to it. If you can't think of anything – make it up!	*If you can dream it, you can do it.*
Have confidence and self-belief		Make sure your inner voice is encouraging and supportive. Be clear what your values are and stick to them. Believe in yourself and your talents.	*Look in the mirror every morning and say 'I'm brilliant!'*
Be persistent and resilient		Never give up, always keep trying even when things are hard. See every mistake as a learning experience.	*If at first you don't succeed, try, try, try again.*
Be an optimist		Look for the positive side of all situations. Speak and walk with your head up and keep a smile on your face.	*Always look on the bright side because your glass is half full, not half empty.*
Take care of yourself – body and brain		Get enough sleep. Don't damage your body with drugs and drink. Keep fit – take exercise. Keep growing your brain by learning every day.	*I'm worth looking after.*
Practise self discipline and willpower		Get in the habit of waiting for things. Have useful self talks that make you realise the best things are worth waiting for.	*No pain, no gain.*
Have courage		Don't stay in your comfort zone. Talk to someone you don't know; take a different route to school, read a new book or newspaper. Have the courage to make changes in your life if you need to.	*Do something that scares you every day. (As long as it's good for you!)*
Co-operate and communicate		Always work with new people and be open and friendly. Compliment and be kind to others. What you give will come back to you.	*Listen and learn – look out for people that have it all and copy them.*
Prioritise and plan		Make lists of what you need to do and get it done. Plan out your activity and take control of your life.	*Do the worst first!*
Total score			
Targets: Pick out your lowest score, copy the text into the boxes			

What have you learnt about EQ?

What have you learnt about EQ? – Teaching it to others is the best way to embed the learning.

By the end of this lesson students will be able to teach a 4-year-old everything they know about EQ.

Plan

Complete the review sheet to ensure understanding. As teaching is the best way of deepening learning, students can prepare and deliver a lesson that covers as much of the content of this section as possible.

In pairs or groups, students will design a poster that covers all aspects of EQ. It will need lots of pictures for a 4-year-old to understand. They can include some drama and other entertainment for the children within their presentation.

Each group presents it to the class who role-play being 4-year-olds – asking questions and so on.

An alternative is to prepare the presentation for a younger year group and deliver it to them.

Prizes can be given for the best presentations.

What have you learnt about EQ?

Write down five things you have learnt about EQ.

1._____

2._____

3._____

4._____

5._____

Write down three things that you would like to improve about your EQ and say how you will do it.

TARGET   HOW

1._____   _____

2._____   _____

3._____   _____

NOW:

1. On a large piece of paper create a colourful design that shows all you have learnt about the habits of EQ over the past few weeks. Imagine using it to teach children of 4 years old all about EQ and how much they need it.

2. Produce a job advertisement for a teacher for your school that will attract someone who has high levels of EQ.

When you have completed it present it to the class and show how you would use it to teach the children.

Lessons in Learning to Learn

Aims

In this section students will learn more about their brain and how to use it more effectively to fulfil their amazing potential.

Amazing Brains

Aims

- To give students an understanding of the latest research on the brain.

- To excite students about the power and potential of their brain to learn.

- To develop skills in thinking that will create positive learning experiences.

Understanding your amazing brain

Resources

Large paper and coloured pens and pencils for spider diagram. A large model of the brain adds to the fun!

Aims

By the end of this lesson students will know more about their brain and how powerful it is.

First thoughts

The quiz on facts about the brain gives a chance to explore myths and truths. The answer to all of the questions is TRUE.

Plan

The bee's brain task asks student to think about all the work a bee's brain does (monitoring time and place, sniffing out pollen, making honey, flying, landing on flowers and so on) with a brain the size of a pinhead. This prepares students to create a spider diagram of all a human brain has to do. This is best completed in pairs on large paper. Please encourage the use of colour and pictures as well as words.

Review

At the end of each lesson students should review three main points they have learnt and share them with a friend.

Extension

Use the Internet to research more facts about the brain.

Understanding your amazing brain

Brain quiz – are these statements true or false?

1. Your brain has more than 100 billion neurons (brain cells).

2. You learn by making connections between these neurons.

3. All your neurons joined together would stretch from here to the moon.

4. Your brain needs plenty of oxygen and water to function properly.

5. If you don't use it, you lose it.

6. Your brain is the size of a large melon.

7. Your brain uses up 20% of your energy.

8. Learning makes your brain more powerful.

9. Your brain is more powerful than a computer the size of the Empire State Building.

10. If brain cells were trees in the Amazon rain forest and neural connections were the leaves, it would take 3 million years to count all the leaves.

A bee has 900 brain cells and a brain the size of a grain of salt

Now write a list of all the things a bee's brain has to think about to survive:

Brainstorm all the things _your_ brain has to do in a large learning map

Your P.E.T. brain

teacher's notes

Resources

Pens and lined paper. Brain model or diagrams. Ask the science department!

Aim

By the end of this lesson students will understand that there are 3 parts to the brain, and what the reptilian part of the brain does.

First thoughts

How do you feel when you are angry?

Plan

The triune brain theory was developed by Dr Paul McClean in 1952. He suggests that there are three parts to the brain:

P – Primitive/Reptilian – monitoring personal survival and 'fight or flight' instinct.

E – Emotional/Limbic System – in the centre of the brain responsible for memory, emotion, values etc.

T – Thinking/Neo Cortex – the thinking cap where higher order thinking skills and speech take place.

This is a useful model for students and teachers trying to make sense of the way they learn.

The P.E.T. acronym makes it easy to remember.

> **TIP: Get students to make a 'brain' by holding both fists together with two thumbs pointing towards their chests. Envisage the thumbs as the reptilian brain stem. Open them up and inside they can see the fingers and wiggle them, demonstrating their emotional brain. The fingers on top represent the 'thinking cap' where all the hard work takes place. However, all three are inextricably linked together and need each other for learning.**

What would you do if…could be developed into brief role-plays with two different reactions. For example:
What would you do if you saw someone smaller being bullied?

Punch the bully
or
Try to reason with him

Which is more likely to get *you* into trouble.

If a written exercise is required then the police statement in Task 2 enables students to think through the consequences of 'reptilian' action.

Finally, the Tasks 1 and 2 are essential for transferring the learning to life experiences. They can be written on paper in large and colourful letters to be displayed at home.

Review

What does P.E.T. stand for and mean?

Share your favourite anger controlling slogan with the class.

Extension

Practise controlling your reptilian brain state as often as possible and teach it to your parents if they lose their temper!

Your P.E.T. brain

P is for Primitive – Reptilian brain

Primitive brain

Emotional brain

Thinking brain

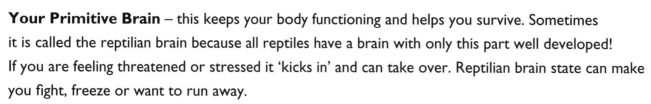

Primitive brain (reptilian)

Emotional brain (limbic)

Thinking brain (Neo-cortex)

Your Primitive Brain – this keeps your body functioning and helps you survive. Sometimes it is called the reptilian brain because all reptiles have a brain with only this part well developed! If you are feeling threatened or stressed it 'kicks in' and can take over. Reptilian brain state can make you fight, freeze or want to run away.

Look at this example:

> Andy was on lesson report so he was working hard on his Maths. The teacher popped out of the room and just as she came back in a ruler went flying past her head. Andy looked up and she accused him of throwing it. He went reptilian. He shouted back at her, slammed his fist on the desk and got sent to the Head.

Discuss or write down an alternative reaction for Andy

What would *you* do …

- If a teacher picked on you unfairly?

- If you are challenged by your parents about using the phone or computer too much?

- If you saw someone small being bullied?

- If you saw the wing of the aeroplane you were travelling in was on fire?

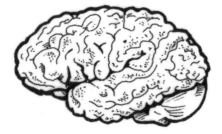

ROAD RAGE is an example of when adults go into reptilian brain state. What do you think happens and why?

Your P.E.T. brain

TASK I

Think of 3 examples of situations when you or someone you know went 'reptilian'.

1. _____

2. _____

3. _____

TASK 2

You are being interviewed by police concerning an incident where you lost your temper.

Explain or write down your version of events.

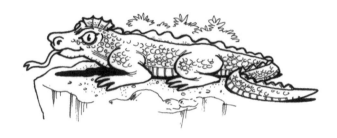

_____

_____

_____

_____

WHAT TO DO IF YOU FEEL REPTILIAN?

1. Write down here 3 ways to calm down and make a positive outcome more likely.

1. _____

2. _____

3. _____

2. Write a set of slogans to say to yourself to control anger.

_____

_____

_____

_____

_____

LESSON 28

Your Emotional Brain

Aim

By the end of this lesson students will understand more about their emotional brain and how to use it to help become a good learner.

Resources

Lined paper, emotional music.

First thoughts

What is your earliest memory?
(It will always be something emotional.)

Plan

Review P.E.T. brain theory.
Play a piece of emotional music that they will recognise such as *Nessun Dorma*, *You'll never walk alone*, *Angels*. Discuss how it makes them feel. Discuss the childhood memories (give some of your own!).
Do the nursery rhyme task to show how music and rhyme help you remember things.
Use the sheet to write down favourite teachers and why they appeal to the emotional brain. This could extend to the least favourite teaching styles and possibilities of why they don't appeal to the emotional brain.

The emotional brain is vital in learning so the four tips need to be discussed and copied down into books or onto posters.

When writing the success story at the end of this lesson it is important that this isn't an English exercise but a visualisation of how good life could be. It can be written or spoken but it must be EXTREME. The emotional brain responds much better to an extremely positive picture so they can make it a ridiculously wonderful day! These can be shared later.

Review

List 5 things the emotional brain responds well to.

Extension

Write a regular diary and each evening predict how tomorrow will be. Use positive goals and events. See if any of them come true!

teacher's notes

Your Emotional Brain

Your P.E.T. Brain – E is for Emotional brain

The limbic system

This part of your brain runs your emotions. It also stores memories and sets your values and beliefs. It is very important in learning. It's much easier to remember emotional experiences than facts. Try it.

- Recall your earliest childhood memory and share it with a partner.

- Now write down any nursery rhyme or songs you can remember from you childhood.

Your emotional brain loves praise, music, rhyme, colour, humour, novelty, enthusiasm and needs to see the point of learning.

- Which are your favourite lessons and teachers? Why?

- Can you link them to your emotional brain?

Learning is emotional...

1. Make it exciting, colourful, funny, and musical. Think of ways to do this with tests coming up … *now*.

2. Give yourself a reason for learning. As long as *you* care, it will count.

3. Set yourself goals for learning and reward your efforts.

4. Use your imagination to help you become a better learner.

5. Use your imagination to help you be more successful at sport or when performing.

Many famous sports stars train in their 'heads', visualising a superb performance to make it happen.

How can you use your emotional brain to help you learn?

TASK

Write your success story *now*. Describe a day in your life when everything goes brilliantly and you are a superstar – especially at learning. Start like this:

'I woke up and the sun was shining. I felt great about the day ahead because…

It doesn't matter if your story seems unlikely or impossible. The more extreme you make it the better!

Now act out your day in groups of 3 or 4.

The Thinking Brain

Resources

Coloured pens and lined/plain paper.

Aim

By the end of this lesson students will know more about the 'thinking' brain and how the 'left' and 'right' brain work together to make a genius. The left and right brain concept is just a metaphor, as activities do not take place in the different areas. It is just an easy way to understand some of the different ways we have of thinking. It can help students to understand how they may need to train their brains to be more logical or more creative.

First thoughts

Ask the students to do some mental arithmetic or difficult spellings. Then ask which part of the brain they think they are using.

Background

The 'thinking' brain loves challenge, instant feedback, making connections and seeing patterns. The brain has two hemispheres and, according to Sperry and Ornstein's Nobel Prize winning theories of 'left-right' brain lateralisation in the 1960s and 1970s, each hemisphere has a different function. This is obviously an oversimplification of a hugely complex process. However, it is still important to help students understand that 'Gestalt' or wholeness means enabling connections. There is much anecdotal evidence that 'right' brain learners find traditional academic education more challenging.

Plan

Use the two fists together activity to remind the students of the parts of the P.E.T. brain, then break them apart to show the 'thinking' brain is in two-halves – left and right.

Discuss the activities shown for each half and how important it is to make them both work together to create really good learning. Students can link each point with a line to show how one helps the other, for example 'imagination' and 'writing'.

The little test is simply a way of finding out if students have strong hemisphere dominance. It must be stressed that there are no right or wrong answers.

Discuss the learning health check and students can note down advice they think may be useful to remember.

Tip

At this point do some brain booster work (Lesson 30) to remind them that this involves the left and right brain working together.

For the task students should use colour, pictures and words to show the right and left activities. This can be completed on A4 or on larger paper.

Review

Explain to your neighbour how the right and left brain work together.

Extension

Use the library to research the neo-cortex.

Review of section

Students should complete this now and feedback to the teacher what they have found most/least useful.

The Thinking Brain

Your P.E.T. Brain – T is for Thinking brain

This is your 'thinking cap' where all the hard work takes place. The brain is sometimes thought of as divided into hemispheres which deal with different things.

Two Halves Make You Whole

LOGICAL (left)	CREATIVE (right)
Writing	Ideas
Logic	Intuition
Numbers	Daydreams
Analysing	Sport
Reading	Playing music
Sequencing	The big picture
Language	Rhythm
Detail	Colour
Spelling	Imagination

These different ways of thinking need to work together to make best use of our brains. For example, when we are doing a jigsaw puzzle we sort out the pieces using colour and shape, but we also have to think about the 'big picture' and imagine how it all fits together to get it right.

To help understand the way your brain works – answer these questions:

Yes or No.

Score: Yes _____ /10

No _____ /10

More Yes than No?
You may be more of a
left-brain thinker.

		Yes	No
1.	I organise facts and material well	☐	☐
2.	I work step by step	☐	☐
3.	I can be impatient	☐	☐
4.	I read instructions before starting	☐	☐
5.	I like to work things out on paper	☐	☐
6.	I like working on my own	☐	☐
7.	I like to make lists	☐	☐
8.	I can concentrate well	☐	☐
9.	I like reading	☐	☐
10.	I enjoy working with numbers	☐	☐

The Thinking Brain

Now answer these questions Yes or No.

Score: Yes _____ /10

No _____ /10

11. I prefer variety and excitement   Yes ☐ No ☐

12. I like to doodle a lot   Yes ☐ No ☐

13. I love trying new ideas   Yes ☐ No ☐

> More Yes than No?
> You may be more of a
> right-brain thinker.

14. I think of creative solutions   Yes ☐ No ☐

15. I like new experiences   Yes ☐ No ☐

16. I just try out ideas as I go along   Yes ☐ No ☐

17. I prefer to flick through a magazine starting at the back Yes ☐ No ☐

18. I make decisions based on gut feelings   Yes ☐ No ☐

19. I find it hard to concentrate quite often   Yes ☐ No ☐

20. I prefer art to reading and maths   Yes ☐ No ☐

> If you have a fairly equal number of yes/no answers you are in the middle, which is an excellent place to be because you are using both sides of your brain for learning!

Learning health check

Using ALL of your brain can make you more clever, so once you know which way you tend to think watch out for these health warnings …

Tips for Left brainers:

● You may need to be more open to trying new approaches.

● Don't get bogged down in detail.

● Practise working well with others.

● Vary your learning styles and habits to keep your creative brain working.

Tips for Right brainers:

● Remember the details – one step at a time.

● Make yourself do some planning and prioritising in advance.

● Avoid procrastination (putting things off!).

● Avoid distraction and distracting others.

● Don't rush in without thinking.

● Read the instructions and check your work when finished.

Get into the habit of using your right and left-brain during learning.

This will make you very intelligent!

● How could you use more right-brain thinking in maths?

● How could you use more left-brain thinking in drama or art?

TASK

● Fill in the two halves of a brain diagram with different activities in right and left hemispheres.

Brain Boosters

Background

This lesson can be done at any time in the first section. It is shown here because it follows on from the left and right brain thinking lesson. The exercises should be repeated every 20-30 minutes – or any time a physical break is needed. The idea is to get the right and left-brain working together and sharpen up the brain's responses. Research has shown many benefits to using these types of exercises in the classroom and students definitely enjoy them!

Resources

Plain paper, coloured pens or preferably individual white boards and markers.

Aim

By the end of this lesson students will know how to boost their brain for learning whenever they need to.

Plan

Practise each movement through once or twice.

Move on to the pen and paper exercises.

These are best done on a whiteboard if possible.

Students can then create some of their own ideas for brain boosters.

They should then choose their favourite brain boosters to write into planners/homework diaries.

Finish by doing the visualisation exercise.

This can be repeated for agility, for example by doing a wonderful dance or gymnastic display.

Review

Students suggest brain booster ideas with the whole class to try, then discuss how they can help boost brain power.

Extension

Try these at home and teach them to members of your family.

Tip

Use some of these exercises on a regular basis (every 20 minutes) in all Learning to Learn (L2L) and other lessons to provide some kinesthetic activity.

Brain Boosters

Warm up for Learning

The brain works best when the two sides, left and right, work together. Here are some ways of getting the left brain and right brain working well to warm up for learning!

- Stand up, stretch, reach up and breathe deeply to give your brain oxygen.

- Rub your tummy with one hand, pat your head with the other.

- Do the twist – arms one way, legs the other way.

- Lift your knee and touch it with the opposite hand. Alternate quickly.

- Draw a large figure of eight in the air with one finger. Draw another large figure eight with the other finger going the other way – make sure your fingers don't touch!

- Trace out the number 10, in the air with one hand creating the 1 and the other hand. Try it with 27, 39 and your age.

- With one hand trace a circle moving outwards from your body. Use the other hand to trace a circle inwards towards your body. Keep them both going at the same time.

- Put your fingertips together very lightly and imagine connections being made between the right and left sides of your brain.

- Fold your arms one way then the other way – repeat until it feels comfortable each way.

- Make your hands into fists and put these together to form a shape that resembles your brain. Blow some energy and power into the gap between your thumbs.

In the air or on paper:

- Write your full name with your wrong hand in large letters.

- Write your name with both hands, creating a mirror image.

- Try writing your name backwards with your wrong hand.

- Write your favourite band, country, and food – using your wrong hand.

- Create an impressive signature then copy with your wrong hand.

- Throw your pen from one hand to the other and back again.

> Boost your brain by trying something new every day. A food you don't eat, a TV programme you never watch, a person you don't usually speak to – make new connections!

Brain Boosters

Have a brain/body work out

Imagine that you are at the gym and a huge set of weights is in front of you. IN YOUR MIND, see yourself in full gym kit looking strong and happy bending your knees and picking up the weights. See yourself lift the weights slowly, keeping your back straight. Then raise the weights to your shoulders. Feel the weight, feel your strength. When you are steady lift them above your head and straighten your arms. Feel the weight for a few seconds then place carefully lower them back to your shoulders. Do this ten times then place them carefully back on the floor. This mental exercise can make you stronger in the real world. ('Mind Sculpture' Robertson 1999.)

Review: Your Amazing Brain

Write down five things you have learnt in Section 2:1, Amazing Brains (Lessons 24–30)

1. _____

2. _____

3. _____

4. _____

5. _____

Write down three action points for you from this section.

1. _____

2. _____

3. _____

Share these ideas with a partner. Put this sheet on your bedroom wall.

Multisensory Learning

Background to this section

Aim

- To raise awareness about the sensory nature of learning.

- To help students understand their own learning preferences and how these impact on learning.

- To provide advice and practical strategies to improve learning through all the senses.

Background

Dr Vernon Magnesen of the University of Texas found in his research about memory that we remember:

10% of what we read
20% of what we hear
30% of what we see
50% of what we see and hear
70% of what we say
90% of what we say and do

Vernon A. Magnesen (1983)

The fact that learning needs to be rehearsed in three different sensory modalities visual, auditory and kinesthetic (VAK) seems like common sense and is the basis of all good lesson planning. Understanding that we all have different preferences in learning derives from the discipline of NLP (neuro-linguistic programming). The way we make sense of the world around us is important in our own communication and learning preferences. As teachers we have learning preferences which affect the way we teach and how students respond to us. By ensuring we teach using all three VAK approaches we will be more successful in engaging all the class in learning.

Making this theory explicit to students will enable them to discover their preferences. However, the purpose of this section is to ensure that they expand their learning capabilities by developing a wider range of learning strategies. Students must not be tempted to categorise themselves simply as 'kinesthetic learners', then expect teachers to adapt all lessons to become practical experiences. To become independent learners for life, students and teachers need first to understand their preferences, then create flexibility in learning by working in and outside of their sensory preference, thus creating those new connections. For a student, understanding why they find it hard to listen may help in realising they need to develop that skill.

See Sense. How to use your senses for learning

Aim

The key message is that we need to keep growing the flexibility of our brain to become better learners. It's not 'I'm kinesthetic so I always need to do practical work. It's 'How can I learn in a variety of ways to help me learn more effectively'.

First thoughts

The first part of the lesson focuses on the senses and what they are.
Through this activity help students understand how we learn through the senses.

Plan

Students can make an initial assessment of their learning preferences through ticking the boxes.

The questionnaire aims to check out learning preferences more objectively to find out if there is a strong tendency towards a visual, auditory or kinesthetic style of learning.

It is important to emphasise that being balanced in all three styles is an excellent place to be because it means that you can be a very flexible learner. In fact (according to anecdotal research), by the time they reach sixth form, successful students have learnt to be more 'equal' in their preferences.

Review

Each student can tell their neighbour their preference and what it means.

Extension

Try to get students to be conscious of their learning over the next week and see the part the senses play in it.

See Sense

How to use your senses for learning

We experience everything we learn through our five senses.

Seeing, Hearing, Touching, Tasting, Smelling

Can you think of anything you experienced that didn't involve the senses?

How did your last lesson smell??

First thoughts

Dogs use their sense of smell to decide who they like and who is a threat.
Think of five ways in which dogs demonstrate their powerful sense of smell.

Blind people show a remarkable development in their other senses.
How can blind people use other senses to 'see'?

We have already discovered that our brains are like our fingerprints – they are all different.
Our multiple intelligences show how we all have different skills and strengths.
This is because we all learn in different ways.

As adults we mainly use three senses for learning – see, hear and touch but we tend to have a preference for learning using one of the three senses.

Preferred learning styles

VISUAL   prefer to learn by seeing, looking at pictures …

AUDITORY   prefer to learn by listening to sounds, going to lectures, taking part in discussions …

KINESTHETIC   prefer to learn by 'hands-on' experience, engaging physically with the world …

You need to know if *you* have a learning preference because it can affect your success if you depend too much on one learning sense. Your challenge is to be good at using all three for learning.

See Sense

Tick which of these apply to you:

VISUAL LEARNERS	AUDITORY LEARNERS	KINESTHETIC LEARNERS
● Have a neat and tidy workplace ☐	● Talk to themselves ☐	● Like physical activity ☐
● Have good presentation skills ☐	● Tell jokes ☐	● Like to make things ☐
● Plan ahead ☐	● Like speeches and singing out loud ☐	● Use gestures ☐
● Like to look good ☐	● Prefer verbal instructions ☐	● Fidget and find it hard to sit still ☐
● Enjoy pictures and maps ☐	● Are distracted by noise ☐	● Need to *do* things to remember them ☐
● Don't always listen well ☐	● Listen well ☐	● Enjoy sport, drama, dance ☐
● Daydream a lot ☐	● Enjoy rhyme/ rhythm ☐	● Like action and action words ☐
● Draw, scribble and doodle ☐	● Discuss and argue well ☐	● Say 'I'll handle that' ☐
● Say 'I see what you mean' ☐	● Say 'Sounds great to me' ☐	● Are easily distracted ☐
TOTAL /9	/9	/9

See Sense

Now check out your sensory preference using this questionnaire:

Tick which of the alternatives below applies most closely to your preference for learning.

Add the scores from page 112 to these.

I like:	SEEING Visual	HEARING Auditory	DOING Kinesthetic
To learn through:	pictures/diagrams/ video ☐	listening to teachers, tapes or people speaking ☐	practical activity ☐
To spell by:	seeing the word in my mind ☐	sounding out the letters ☐	writing the word out a number of times ☐
To relax through:	watching TV, sport or films ☐	listening to music or the radio ☐	playing games or sport ☐
To learn a foreign language through:	looking at cards, posters, videos and books ☐	listening to tapes and saying the words ☐	playing games and role-plays ☐
To learn a new sport by:	watching a demonstration ☐	listening to instructions and talking to a coach ☐	playing it ☐
To learn in science by:	looking at diagrams in books and teacher demonstrations ☐	listening to a teacher talking ☐	doing practical experiments ☐
To remember events by:	seeing images, scenes, faces and colours ☐	hearing sounds, words or music ☐	focusing on action and feelings about the event ☐
To write:	descriptive passages ☐	speech and dialogue ☐	action stories ☐
To find out information by:	looking in books ☐	asking an expert and listening to them ☐	surfing the worldwide web ☐
Which describes you best?	I like to plan ahead and see the future ☐	I sometimes talk or sing to myself ☐	I get restless if I sit still for too long ☐
TOTAL SCORES IN EACH COLUMN:	/10	/10	/10
OVERALL SCORE	V /19	A /19	K /19

Are you an auditory, visual or kinesthetic learner?

We all use all of our senses so many of you will be balanced between two or all three categories.

Use as many senses as possible to make learning more memorable.

Be a powerful visual learner

Aim

By the end of this lesson students will understand how to improve their visual learning. Start by warming up your visual learning muscles by visualising and understanding how they work.

First thoughts

'Imagine a cat sitting on your lap...' This helps students locate how and whether they can see pictures in their minds. If some students can't see the cat then they may need extra help in developing visualisation techniques.

Plan

The learning maps are topics which students can grow and develop in a spider diagram format. They should be colourful, contain key words *and* pictures, in order to be brain friendly. Apart from this there are no strict rules and students should be encouraged to develop their own style. They are really useful for revising topics or mapping what students already know.

Some (especially left brainers) may find them hard and frustrating – because they are developing parts of their brain that they are not used to using – good! Some will say 'I can't draw' but this exercise is not about creating a work of art and the sillier and funnier it is, the better. It will be more memorable.

Starting with YOU for the first map means all students can achieve. Alternatively, you could revise the work so far on this course by producing a learning maps about the brain.

The idea is to make a map using key words *then* create it using pictures. The pictures can be simple and symbolic. (Hence the picture exercise.) Then the words are added to create the perfect brain-friendly learning map.

If there is time to try this with topics from other lessons this is most beneficial.

Review

Tell a neighbour how learning maps can help you learn.

> 'Imagination is everything. It is the preview of life's coming attractions'.
>
> *Albert Einstein*

Be a powerful visual learner

Use your eyes to see and use your mind to create visual pictures

You have discovered you learning sensory preference. But the best learners use *all* their senses to learn. Whatever your preference for learning you need to develop *each* of your senses for powerful learning.

First thoughts

Imagine a cat sitting on your lap. See yourself stroking it, see its colour and feel its texture. What colour is the cat?

If you find it hard to visualise the cat, then you need to practise using internal visualising for learning!

Learning maps

Creating a learning map involves writing down all the important information you need to know but writing it down in a way that is brain friendly and that captures your visual imagination. Most of the time we write our notes in lists and paragraphs. This does not always help us remember them. Good learning maps use:

COLOUR

PICTURES

SYMBOLS AND IMAGES

WORDS

These are all brain friendly and give us visual stimulation.

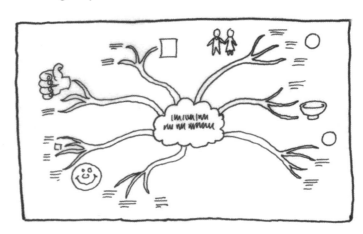

Be a powerful visual learner

Learning maps start with a central idea and grow branches in all directions as ideas flow. It doesn't matter if they are not artistic or organised.

Start this learning map on yourself. Start in the middle of the sheet of paper with the key word you are going to use to grow your ideas from. Draw a box containing the word 'ME' and then add – radiating out from this central point – where you live, what type of house, people in your family, pets, your personality, your hobbies and so on.

It doesn't matter how untidy it is – just get as much information down as you can. You can always redraw it later when themes and patterns emerge – and this will assist your learning. Don't put any pictures in this map.

Here are some simple drawings – what does each one mean to you? Draw a learning map for each one.

Be a powerful visual learner

Pictures can be simple and easy to draw. You need to use simple pictures and images in your learning maps – but you don't have to be an artist.

Make a pictorial learning map

Now on a larger piece of paper convert your learning map about yourself into a map made entirely of colourful symbols, pictures, cartoons and diagrams. They can be as simple and silly as you like.

Add the words from your first map after you have finished all the pictures.

Add a title – **now you have a learning map with words and pictures that is easy to learn from.**

Give it to a neighbour to study for 5 minutes – then test how much they have learnt about you.

Ask them how they remembered bits of the map. Was it through the pictures or the words? Did they see the map inside their heads? If they did they were using their visual memory.

Now create a learning map for a science topic or for a book you are studying. Remember to use lots of key words, colours and pictures.

It is *your* learning map, so it doesn't matter if it isn't neat or tidy as long as **you** understand it.

From now on:

Look in on your internal visual learning cinema. Spend time enjoying daydreaming, reliving happy times and rerunning good lessons that helped you learn.

Also,

- Ask your teachers if you can map your notes in your book if that helps you to learn. Visual, right brain learners learn better from mind maps.

- Use learning maps to revise for tests.

- Use learning maps to plan and organise yourself.

- Try mapping on the computer using www.mindman.com.

LESSON 33

Using your inner eye

Aim

By the end of this lesson students will understand more about their visual memory and how to use it to make them better learners.

First thoughts

The mind-body connection is a task to help students understand that thinking things makes you feel things too!

The next tasks ask you the teacher to take students through some visualisation tasks and then represent them in a learning map. This is to hone up their visualisation skills. For some students this will be challenging but it is vital that they start to practise visualisation.

Some students will not be used to being asked to see things in their head so expect a little unease at first. However, visual learning is the most powerful and this lesson will help explain that to students.

After the first exercises give students some simple mental arithmetic and spelling problems so that they can think about how they process this information. For example, spell 'disappear' – did you see it, hear it or sound it out? For example, what is 23 times 2? How are you accessing the answer? Are you seeing the sum in your head?

The lesson remembering task can be done using the whiteboard with rewards for those that remember the most in 30 seconds.

The moving eye test is for fun but also to focus on how we access our visual memory by 'looking' into certain areas of our brain. The questions are constructed to elicit a variety of created and remembered thoughts.

<u>Upward</u> eye movements to the <u>left</u> indicate REMEMBERED <u>sights</u> or scenes.

<u>Upward</u> eye movements to the <u>right</u> indicate CONSTRUCTED OR CREATED <u>visual</u> scenes.

<u>Level</u> eye movements to the <u>left</u> indicate REMEMBERED <u>sounds</u>.

<u>Level</u> eye movements to the <u>right</u> indicate CONSTRUCTED OR CREATED <u>sounds</u>.

Tip

Students will find it interesting that some management companies use eye movements to detect if an applicant is lying about his CV!

Use whiteboards to record eye movements in previously drawn eyes.

Students can create questions that may involve lies in order to check eye movement out.

teacher's notes

Create your own virtual reality

This task is best done initially as a guided visualisation by the teacher to show students how to do it. Put the relaxing music on and get them to imagine a scene where there is a big sports or pop event. Build up the sights and sounds of the scene slowly and carefully focusing on wonderful sunshine, happiness and excitement. Make them see it as a cinema screen, big, colourful and noisy (use all the senses). Then as the scene evolves the star of the show is them, performing to everyone's acclaim.

We all mentally rehearse events, often in a negative way which programmes our brain to fail. The purpose of this exercise is to show students how to make a powerful visual picture that can have a positive effect on performance. Just by practising visualisation, students will acquire the skill and be able to use it on demand.

Review

Students read the tips for visual learning and discuss with a partner how many of these things they do already.

Using your inner eye

The cinema screen that is your mind

First thoughts

Do you remember in words or pictures?

Developing your visual learning involves being able to create pictures in your mind and then using them to help you learn.

- Imagine a puppy sitting on the desk in front of you

- Write down exactly what it looks like and what it is doing. See yourself playing with it and picking it up.

- Now change the puppy into a snake. Does this feel different?

Imagining things can make you feel physical effects!

These visual memories are very important in learning. Try some mental arithmetic – do you see it in your head?

In pairs:

How good is your inner eye?

Describe the walls of this classroom without looking at them.

Recall your last lesson – describe in as much detail what you can see in your mind.

Each pair give a mark out of ten for the amount their partner can remember.

Now recall the best lesson/experience you ever had – make the picture in your head bright and colourful and as big as a cinema screen.
Describe it to each other in pairs.
How does it make you feel to see it in your head?
Draw a spider diagram/doodle of that lesson with images and words that capture the atmosphere.

Spell out a word – do you see it first?

TASK

1. Put some lively, familiar music on. Write down or draw all the visual images that come into your head.

2. Write a paragraph about how visualising in your head helps **you** to learn.

Using your inner eye

Did you know your eyes move when you are visualising something in your head?

The moving eye test

Look straight at a partner and ask these questions. Fill in which direction the eyes move for each answer.

What colour is your front door? _____

Imagine seeing a purple lion. _____

How many people and animals live at your house? _____

What would I look like with blue hair? _____

What would an elephant squeaking sound like? _____

Think of your favourite song and listen to it in your head. _____

Your eyes move to a different place when they look in your head for information or try to imagine something. Make up four more questions to test out eye movement.

Create your own virtual reality

Give your visual imagination a workout every day by daydreaming a situation where you are the hero of a success story.

Try it now – put some soft music on and set the scene in your head. This works even better if you do the relaxation exercise first. (Lesson 13)

Now draw a picture **or** write an account of this story to remind yourself.

Tips for visual learning

- Put posters, charts, key words and your learning maps on your bedroom wall.

- Use lots of colour, and highlighter pens in your notes, especially for key words and concepts.

- Watch videos, read books – especially illustrated books. Use interactive software or the internet to help you learn.

- Develop your listening skills and make sure you take part in any practical activities. Don't just sit and watch!

- Take some time out to regularly visualise and rerun all your best lessons and best moments. Do this just before you go to sleep for maximum impact!

Improve literacy through visualisation

Aim

Much research has been done in the USA (notably by Lindamood–Bell, www.lblp.com) on the correlation between a failure to create visual images and restricted comprehension skills. This lesson helps students use imaging to understand text.

First thoughts

Teachers should get students to recall memories of holidays and describe them in some detail to start to locate the visual memory.

Plan

First read out the passage and then students can produce the images in the boxes for each section. It really doesn't matter whether they use pictures, colours or words in each box as long as they are focusing on the images. It is much better if they talk about what they are seeing and describe it in detail.

For the Shakespeare piece students can talk through or draw images that come to mind with each line to help them learn what it means and possibly learn it off by heart. Experiment with other texts.

(Please pass on this technique to your Literacy Co-ordinator because it could really help students improve their reading skills.)

> 'Man's mind cannot understand thoughts without images of them'.
>
> *Thomas Aquinas*

Improve literacy through visualisation

Turn movies on in your head when you read

'Man's mind cannot understand thoughts without images of them' *Thomas Aquinas*

Visualising for comprehension

If you can make pictures in your mind it can help you understand what you read and this will help you in exams.

Read this passage from 'Unforgettable places to see before you die' by Steve Davey.

1. As you stand in the cold darkness of an Arizona night, waiting for dawn, you will have no comprehension of the enormity of the landscape in front of you. In the dull early light your first view of the Grand Canyon will be a flat, almost painterly composition.

2. Then gradually the sky turns to blue and red, and golden sunlight starts to pick out details – first the edge of the far ridge, then the tallest pinnacles inside the canyon itself.

3. As the sun rises higher, more is revealed. Rock formations sculpted by years of erosion are illuminated, and long, convoluted shadows are cast on to giant screens formed by cliffs.

4. Only when you notice the details, such as a row of trees, or a flock of geese flying overhead, do you come to realise the true scale of the canyon. That far ridge might be 15km away, and the mighty Colorado River – a mere stream viewed from above – is 1500 metres below.

Improve literacy through visualisation

For each section 1–4

Create a picture in your head.

In each box either write words or draw pictures or stick men to show what is in these pictures.

Add extra details that make it more interesting but still fits with the text.

Describe in words what is in each picture to your neighbour.

1	2

3	4

Improve literacy through visualisation

Test how this has improved your memory and understanding by describing what is in the passage below.

Make it into a film.

Making visual images can help you understand and remember poetry.

Create a picture for each section of this famous speech in Shakespeare's 'Macbeth'.

1. 'Tomorrow and tomorrow and tomorrow
   Creeps in this petty pace from day to day
   To the last syllable of recorded time

2. And all our yesterdays have lighted fools the
   way to dusty death. Out, out brief candle!
   Life's but a walking shadow, a poor player
   That struts and frets his hour upon the stage
   And then is heard no more;

3. It is a tale
   Told by an idiot, full of sound and fury
   Signifying nothing'

Describe to your neighbour what is in each picture and why.

See how much of the poem and its meaning you can now remember.

The more you practise visualising and talking about those pictures the easier you will find it to remember things and understand meanings.

1

2

3

The best learners are listeners – Auditory Learning

Aims

By the end of this lesson students will understand how to be a better listener and improve their auditory learning skills.

First thoughts

Students are asked to listen very carefully to sounds around them to get in touch with what it means.

Whiteboards or paper are good to jot down sounds heard in a timed minute in the classroom.

Take the level of listening further by asking the students to listen to the inner body sounds. This intrigues students and they will come out with interesting suggestions.

The pair work involves paraphrasing and repeating back what has been told. This is important training in counselling work. The role-play tests this ability.

The counselling task could be extended by the teacher describing an imaginary crime. The students listen carefully to the details and then see how much they can remember. An extension of this is to mime a crime, then see whether more is remembered through the visual experience. Have two sixth formers run in and 'steal' your purse or wallet.

Discussing the inner voice/dialogue is a useful exercise and helps students become aware of how they can motivate themselves through self-talk.

Review

Students read the tips for auditory learners and discuss which would work well for you.

Extension

Students:
Teach your parents what you have learnt about multisensory learning.

The best learners are listeners!

Learn with your ears – auditory learning

Some people learn well through listening. Listening is a very important skill to acquire as so much of what we have to learn is presented auditorily by teachers talking to the group, or through group discussions. Therefore, every student needs to have good **listening skills**.

Listen to the sounds around you now – jot down everything you can hear.

_____

_____

_____

_____

Auditory learners say:

Can you hear what I am saying?

That rings a bell with me.

I've heard it all before.

Now listen to your insides – what can you hear?

_____

_____

_____

_____

What makes a good listener?

_____

_____

_____

_____

_____

The best learners are listeners!

How do you know you have heard something?

What mental processes go on after you have heard something important?

In pairs, find out how good you are at listening. Here are some activities that will involve careful listening:

- Listen to a poem read out by the teacher – once. See how many words and phrases from the poem you can remember and jot them down.

- Tell your partner some details of your last holiday – make them repeat back to you the main points.

- Play a piece of music or a pop song and really listen to the words and music. Try singing it afterwards.

Listening skills are vital to learning and to life.

TASK – in pairs

Imagine you are at a counselling session. One of you is the counsellor, one the client. Tell the counsellor your real (or imaginary) problems about school or home in three or four minutes. The counsellor then has to repeat back to you a summary of the problems and suggest some solutions.

We listen in our heads too!

Listen to your internal dialogue – you know the voice that talks to you inside your head. It often gives you a running commentary on what you are doing and what you are going to do. What sort of voice is it? Is it your voice? Change the way it sounds. If it is normally miserable and complaining then make it positive and encouraging. This can be very motivating. How does this change make you feel? What did your inner voice just say? Was it positive?

The best learners are listeners!

Look at this example:

You are asked to do a bungee jump for charity. Two thoughts that may come into your head are:

Internal voice: 'I might die! People get injured. I might chicken out at the last minute and look like a fool.'

Positive voice: 'That could be exciting. I can do it and think how good it would make me feel. I will be making money for someone else.'

Which one is closer to how **you** think?

> Practise now making your internal voice say something positive to you.

Make the most of self-talk to build confidence and self belief

AVOID – Negative self-talk

I can't do it.

She hates me.

I've never been good at exams.

My writing is rubbish.

No one likes me.

It's bound to go wrong.

Add some more.

INCREASE – *Positive self-talk*

I'm brilliant and beautiful!

I can do anything if I work hard enough.

I love exams.

I am an excellent friend.

I am very determined to get it right.

I am born lucky.

Add some more.

TASK

Create a business card with all your positive self-talk statements on it to remind you how to help build your confidence.

Tips for auditory learning:

● Read your notes out loud.

● Make a cassette tape of your notes.

● Make your notes into a rhyme or rap – or even better, sing them!

● Talk out loud to yourself when you are trying to understand something.

● Listen to music while you are working.

● Spell out words by making the sounds out loud.

● Teach other people what you know.

● Listen to your inner voice. Teach it to say positive things about you and about what you are doing.

Kinesthetic Learning

Resources

Small blank cards and coloured pens.

Aim

By the end of this lesson students will have learnt ways to use kinesthetic learning to help them remember things.

First thoughts

What are the five senses and how do they help with learning?

Plan

Emphasise that those with a preference for kinesthetic learning will **tend** to find traditional academic subjects more difficult. However, if they can expand their other sensory learning preferences they will become more successful and flexible. However, the 'doing' part of the learning experience is essential to reinforce learning so this lesson gives some experience of how practical activity can help learning.

The French role-play could be in any language. The focus is on fun and learning vocabulary in a practical way. It is important to test the outcome and see if the words and their meaning have been learnt in this way.

Using cards or Post-its™ for the next exercise is a way of making any factual learning kinesthetic by creating cards with key words on that can be physically moved around. Add pictures and colour to the cards for added sensory impact.

Students should check from the list of kinesthetic activities how many they do and how often.

Review

Read tips for kinesthetic learning and discuss which ones you will do in the next week.

The review of this multisensory learning section can be completed in this lesson and noted in students' books or on the sheet.

Kinesthetic Learning

I can handle that!

Some people learn best by practical activity. Everyone benefits from reinforcing learning by practical activity.

Kinesthetic learners prefer to get on and do things rather than listen to instructions or watch the video.

Although kinesthetic learners find it hard to sit still, they still need to learn through the other senses too. Practise listening and meditating to become an all-round learner.

If you are not inclined towards kinesthetic learning you need to make sure you grab every opportunity for practical activity because this way your brain will keep developing.

Practical exercises do help you learn something more thoroughly.

Role-play helps you learn by doing.

Learn French through role-play

Make up a play using as many of these twelve French words as possible. You can only speak French and the rest of the play must be mimed.

bonjour (hello)	bien (well/good)	chien (dog)
chat (cat)	manger (eat)	maison (house)
eau (water)	au revoir (goodbye)	s'il vous plait (please)
jambon (ham)	fromage (cheese)	jus d'orange (orange juice)

Now test your knowledge of the French vocabulary.

Use cards to help you learn.

Brainstorm in any order the key events and characters from a film or book you have seen or read recently. Write each one on small cards or Post-its™. Organise each card on your desk in the correct order and move them into a pattern you like. Then talk through them to a neighbour.

Now do this again, this time choosing a science topic. For example, the characteristics of living things. Make the key cards and arrange them in the order that makes sense. This way you will learn more effectively than just reading your notes. Try it with a maths method or a food recipe.

Kinesthetic Learning

Try to do some of these kinesthetic activities every week

Dancing	Juggling
All sports, games and the gym	Arts and craft
Pottery	Cooking
Swimming	Cycling
Drama	Gardening

TIPS FOR KINESTHETIC LEARNING

- Make a model of the process.
- Role-play what you have learnt.
- Do regular brain boosters (Lesson 30).
- Go on field trips and visits to enhance learning.
- Use Post-its™ notes to write and draw on.
- Use fingers to count on.
- Doodle while listening.
- Use a stress ball to squeeze.

Kinesthetic learning creates a mind-body connection that can help you remember things.

Be active in your learning. Always volunteer an answer to questions and get involved in the lessons.

Review of MULTISENSORY LEARNING.

Write down five things you have learnt from this section:

1. _____

2. _____

3. _____

4. _____

5. _____

Write down three targets for improving your learning through all your senses.

1. _____

2. _____

3. _____

SECTION 2:3

Multiple Intelligences

Aims

To help students to understand that their are many ways to be clever.

To identify for students their own personal strengths and weak spots.

Background

Howard Gardner's theory of multiple intelligence is more than 20 years old, but recent research supports the idea that there may be zones of activity in the brain that control certain skills and abilities. There were originally seven intelligences: interpersonal, intrapersonal, linguistic, mathemeatical or logical, visual or spacial, physical or kinesthetic, and musical but naturalist was added and now spiritualist is considered to be the ninth intelligence. For the purposes of this section the eight intelligences have been used.

These intellegences are now often referred to as <u>Smarts</u> which are more student friendly:

- People Smart
- Self Smart
- Number Smart
- Picture Smart
- Body Smart
- Music Smart
- Nature Smart

How can I be a genius?

| There are lots of ways to be clever.

Aim

To help students understand that there are lots of ways to be clever and that they need to develop all of their talents. The lesson outlines the 'Smarts' and what they mean in the hope that students will be able to identify some of their talents.

The first thoughts are designed to capture students preconceived ideas of intelligence. By the end of this lesson they will know how many ways there are to be intelligent. Intelligence is not just IQ.

Plan

Students complete the first task, discussing each intelligence and make an initial assessment of their own competences.

The role-play works well when the students are encouraged to make it surreal and imaginative. Students can introduce the brain and act out the different intelligences.

Review

Present role-play to the class. Review the intelligences around the class before they leave.

How can I be a genius?

There are lots of ways to be clever

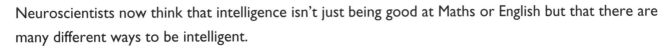

Find out in this section how you are clever in many different ways and how you can use this to improve results.

First thoughts:

What is intelligence?

Name some famous geniuses

What things do very intelligent people do and say?

Neuroscientists now think that intelligence isn't just being good at Maths or English but that there are many different ways to be intelligent.

You have…Multiple Intelligences!

There are lots of ways you are smart. Here are some of them:

Discuss each one with a friend and decide which apply most to you.

Interpersonal   **or**   **People smart**

Are you good at getting on with people – not just your friends but adults, children, teachers? Are you a good listener, showing consideration and tolerance? Do you work well in groups and enjoy meeting new people? Are you generally popular with friends? People smart means you are skilful at getting on with others – you have to have interpersonal intelligence to do this.

Intrapersonal   **or**   **Self smart**

Understanding yourself and the way you work is vital for success in life. Intrapersonal intelligence is about being aware of your feelings and understanding your strengths and weaknesses. Can you control your moods and motivate yourself? Can you explain the way you behave in certain situations? Are you good at setting yourself targets and sticking to promises? If you are then you have a high intrapersonal intelligence.

How can I be a genius?

Linguistic   or   Word smart

If you enjoy reading and talking using a well developed vocabulary you will be word smart. You may be good at writing essays and stories and enjoy playing around with words and meanings. If you are word smart your favourite lesson may be English.

Mathematical and Logical   or   Number smart

Are you good at solving problems and sorting things out in a step by step fashion? Do you make lists of things to do and work through them? Your favourite subjects may be maths and science and you enjoy brainteasers and puzzles. If this sounds like you – you are number smart.

Visual and Spatial   or   Picture smart

Do you think in pictures? If you enjoy drawing, painting and looking at pictures, these are signs of visual/spatial intelligence. Learning more effectively from maps, graphs and pictures is easy for picture smart people.

Physical and Kinesthetic   or   Body smart

This is the ability to use your body skilfully in sport, dance or in building and constructing things. If you are strong in this intelligence you will enjoy lessons like PE, drama and technology. You will enjoy doing things yourself rather than watching others and will sometimes find it hard to sit still!

Musical   or   Music smart

If you have got good rhythm and enjoy singing or playing an instrument you are likely to have a strong musical intelligence. Do you listen to a variety of music because you want to and can you pick out patterns and instruments that others don't seem to notice? This is another sign of being music smart.

How can I be a genius?

Naturalist   or   **Nature smart**

If you are nature smart then you are aware and interested in all plants and animals, insects and rocks and the relationship between them. You may love being outdoors and care about the environment around you. You may be very aware of animal rights issues and hope to have a career in an outdoor environment.

TASK 1

Think of an activity you do that uses each intelligence.

People	Self	Word	Number	Picture	Body	Music	Nature

TASK 2

In groups of 4/5 create a role-play that shows the different intelligences at work in the brain. You can imagine the brain as a huge machine, with the different parts represented by movements or people. Try switching parts off and on. Show your role-play to the group.

How am I smart?

The intelligences students use.

Aim

By the end of this lesson students will have completed a multiple intelligence wheel and know what their strengths are.

First thoughts

The first thoughts are designed to get students to estimate their profile then check it out with a self-assessment test.

Plan

Explain the test and how it relates to previous lessons. Score 5 if the student feels very strongly this statement applies. Encourage students to use the whole range of marks and to be honest.

Mark test scores with students and they will have a total for each intelligence which can be transferred onto the graph. Shade each intelligence in a different colour and produce a key if they wish.

When the graphs are completed they can be cut out and stuck into students books if required.

It is important that students realise that this is a snapshot of their present perceptions and can and should change over time as they grow their brains.

Review

Students report back on their profiles and what they mean to them. Students could also peer-assess each others profiles.

Extension

Take the test home for parents to try.

How am I smart?

The intelligences I use

First thoughts

Guess which you think your top 3 Smarts are and write them here:

Now you may have an idea of which intelligences are your strengths and maybe which are those you need to work on. Complete this questionnaire to check out your scores.

Score yourself with 1–5 marks for each question – 5 being high. Be honest!

1.   I am good at working with objects and making things. ☐

2.   I am good at finding my way around. ☐

3.   I am good at sorting out arguments with friends. ☐

4.   I can remember words to songs easily. ☐

5.   I always do things one step at a time. ☐

6.   I know myself well and understand why I behave the way I do. ☐

7.   I keep/like pets and other animals. ☐

8.   I enjoy socialising with friends. ☐

9.   I learn well from talks and listening to people. ☐

10.   When I listen to music it can change my mood. ☐

11.   I can explain things clearly to people. ☐

12.   I enjoy puzzles, crosswords and logic problems. ☐

How am I smart?

13. I learn a lot from pictures, posters and diagrams. ☐

14. I am sensitive to the moods and feelings of those around me. ☐

15. I learn best when I get up and do it for myself. ☐

16. I prefer to be outside in the open air whenever I can. ☐

17. I learn best when I have set myself a goal. ☐

18. I enjoy peace and quiet for working. ☐

19. When listening to music I can recognise different instruments. ☐

20. I get angry when animals are maltreated or the environment is abused. ☐

21. I can picture places and faces easily in my head. ☐

22. I know a good range of words and I like to learn new ones. ☐

23. I enjoy writing. ☐

24. I have a good sense of balance and enjoy dancing. ☐

25. I can understand graphs and use a calculator properly. ☐

26. I work well in a team or group. ☐

27. I am observant and often see things others don't. ☐

28. I get restless and fidgety easily. ☐

29. I enjoy working on a project by myself. ☐

30. I can recognise different types of birds, trees or plants. ☐

31. I enjoy making music. ☐

32. I am good with numbers and maths. ☐

How am I smart?

Scoring your answers

Intelligence		Score for each question								Total
Interpersonal	People Smart	3	8	14	26					
Intrapersonal	Self Smart	6	17	18	29					
Linguistic	Word smart	9	11	22	23					
Maths/logical	Number smart	5	12	25	32					
Visual/spatial	Picture Smart	2	13	21	27					
Kinesthetic	Body Smart	1	15	24	28					
Musical	Music Smart	4	10	19	31					
Naturalist	Nature Smart	7	16	20	30					

Now fill in the intelligence graph below to see how your scores compare.

	people	self	word	number	picture	body	music	nature

(graph with y-axis values 20, 15, 10, 5 on both left and right sides)

Take control ...

Why are your scores like this? ....

....

What do you need to do to improve your low scores?

....

....

Using all your intelligences

Aim

'Growing your brain by building flexibility'.

The more students practise activities the better they get at flexible learning.
By the end of this lesson students will know how to improve all the different intelligences with practical activities.

First thoughts

Review the graph and recap on the students' intelligences.

Look at the chart and examples. Class discussion on other ideas. Use sheets from Lesson 37 to help.

Pair work to create further ideas.

Share class ideas and complete the chart.

Task

The idea of this task is for students to plan a weekend of learning using all they know about multiple intelligences. Their planning can be in pictures or words but will need to be presented to the class.

Review

Recap ideas for improving each intelligence.

Using all your intelligences

To become a genius you need to work on all your intelligences

Look at your multiple intelligence graph again. Remember:

To become a genius you need to work on ALL your intelligences.

Fill in this chart of things to do to improve each intelligence.

People Smart	Self Smart	Word Smart	Number Smart	Picture Smart	Body Smart	Music Smart	Nature Smart
Listen to others	Think more often!	Learn a new word every day	Practise mental arithmetic and tables	Do jigsaws	Learn to juggle	Play music while you work	Plant something and watch it grow
Smile	Keep a diary	Read more	Do puzzle books	Develop your doodling skills	Learn a dance routine	Sing in the shower	Collect some leaves

TASK

In groups of four using a large piece of paper, plan a weekend away for a group of students. Make a programme of activities that will use all their multiple intelligences and improve them. Make it visual. Use pictures, flow charts or diagrams to show the activities. Make a presentation of your ideas to the rest of the group.

LESSON 40

Learning in different ways

Aim

By the end of this lesson students will have learnt the verses shown from the William Blake poem 'The Tyger' using their strongest intelligence.

First thoughts

How do you usually learn something quickly?

Plan

Group students according to their intelligences but try to make each group no bigger than 5 students.

Each group tries to learn all three verses in 20 minutes.

Students can demonstrate how well they have done by performing the verse to the class.

Review

Discussion on how well it worked trying to learn in different ways.

Now the students add which intelligence they were developing at that time and colour code it.

teacher's notes

Learning in different ways

CHALLENGE

To learn these verses from William Blake's poem 'The Tyger'

Tyger, tyger burning bright
In the forests of the night,
What immortal hand or eye
Could frame thy fearful symmetry?

In what distant deeps or skies
Burnt the fire of thine eyes?
On what wings dare he aspire?
What the hand dare seize the fire?

When the stars threw down their spears,
And watered heaven with their tears,
Did he smile his work to see?
Did he who made the Lamb make thee?

Reproduced with permission of Harper Collins

Working with your best intelligence in pairs or groups of others with the same 'best' intelligence, learn this quotation. Use some of the following techniques.

If you are:

People Smart	Teach each other/test each other, talk about what it means.
Body Smart	Act out the words with actions and mime as you learn it.
Self Smart	Learn it in your head, think about the meaning.
Number Smart	Count the syllables in each line and number the lines. Learn one line at a time with its number.
Word Smart	Find out what each word means and what the story is about. Say the words over and over again out loud.
Picture Smart	Doodle and draw as you say the words. Find a picture to help you remember each line.
Music Smart	Make this into a rap or set it to a musical tune of your choice as you learn it.

Each group perform to the rest of the class to see how well you learnt the passage.

Learn spellings, maths rules, French or German vocabulary, important dates and people, science words, phone numbers – learn them using your intelligences.

Try to use as many of these intelligences as you can whenever you learn.

Challenging your brain to use the Smarts

Aim

Students make the Smarts work for them to make them smarter in all subjects.

First thoughts

Students fill in the timeline from one year old that recalls all big learning occasions in life and then relate them to the Smarts.

By the end of this lesson students will be able to use their best intelligence to improve their weak spots.

Plan

The first task attempts to link intelligences to subjects. When they have listed their favourite subject they can draw a line across to see if there are any links to their best intelligence. Discussion on the sample table could elicit more ideas from students on how to use their skills to break down learning barriers. Completing their own table can be done in their books for more space.

The concluding task: *'Intelligence – what is it all about?'* can be an article, chat show or poster. This acts to consolidate of the learning in this section.

Review of Section 2

This lesson includes a review of the learning in this section which should be completed when all the other activities are finished.

Challenging your brain to use the Smarts

Making the Smarts work for you to make you smarter in all subjects

First thoughts

Fill in this timeline to show how you have grown your intelligence since you were a baby. Put key points when you think you may have grown your brain such as talking, walking, learning to ride a bike, read and so on.

Age 1 year ⟶

Now add which intelligence you were developing at that time and colour code them.

MULTIPLE INTELLIGENCES – how are you smart?

Now you know what your strengths are, learn to use them to make yourself a genius!

List your 5 strongest intelligences here.	List your favourite subjects here.
1.	1.
2.	2.
3.	3.
4.	4.
5.	5.

Do you always tend to spend time and energy on these favourites?

If you do this it will make them stronger.

List your 3 weakest intelligences here.	List the subjects you find hardest here.
1.	1.
2.	2.
3.	3.

Challenging your brain to use the Smarts

Are you working hard to improve your weak spots? This is the way to improve your brain power.

To maximise your brain power you need to use your strongest intelligences for learning AND improve your weak spots.

Show how could you use your strongest intelligence to help you with your weak spots.

Here is an example:

What I need to work on	Using my No 1 Intelligence BODY SMART I will …	Using my No 2 Intelligence MUSIC SMART I will …	Using my No 3 Intelligence PEOPLE SMART I will …
Number smart	Use cards, beads, fingers to help	Make equations into a rap	Teach your friends formulas
Self smart	Start a fitness training programme and learn to set personal, achievable goals	Use music to create your mood and encourage you to think	Ask friends to give you honest opinions about yourself
Word smart	Learn spellings by tracing out the word on the back of your hand	Listen carefully to the lyrics of songs and find out what they mean	Learn new words from friends who are clever with language

NOW TRY COMPLETING THIS TABLE WITH YOUR OWN IDEAS:

What I need to work on	No 1 intelligence	No 2 intelligence	No 3 intelligence

TASK

Create a television chat show or a newspaper article called

INTELLIGENCE – WHAT'S IT ALL ABOUT ANYWAY?

Values for success in life

Aims

This section links to the need for students to develop as 'Responsible Citizens' with beliefs and values that will sustain them through the challenges they may meet in school and in life. Each lesson gives students a chance to think about and determine what matters to them for health, happiness and success. This section has many links to PSHE and Citizenship.

Activities are included here to help students take control of their lives and of their learning by building a core understanding of their values and how to make sure they can live in harmony with what they believe in.

42. What are the values for success in life?
43. **V** is Vote for democracy and equality
44. **A** is for Attitude is everything
45. **L** is for Love is all you need
46. **U** is for Understanding that family and friends matter!
47. **E** is for Enterprise and energy
48. **S** is for Social intelligence
49. **L** is for Laughter and fun
50. **I** is for I can choose
51. **F** is for Forgiveness and Fairness
52. **E** is for Earn respect through Empathy

What are the values for success in life?

This lesson introduces the notion that holding certain values will help to lead to success for our students.

Values are defined as 'human values' to avoid conflict with religious values. However there is lots of overlap.

'Human values, are pillars which develop through an interaction of need, perception, emotion, sentiment and attitude. A value is well defined as an endeavour which satisfies the 'need 'system' (Human Values Foundation).

Our needs drive us to behave in certain ways, so helping students understand which values are important to them will impact on their behaviour and achievement.
The purpose of this section is to help students develop an awareness of what they value and how to use those values to guide their decisions and behaviour.

Throughout this section students should be encouraged to reflect by giving them 'thinking time' – even if it is just for a minute or two at the end of the lesson.

This lesson begins with first thoughts which explore what values are and what students value.

The quiz helps students to reflect on how firmly they hold their values.

The main task takes the acronym (VALUESLIFE) and firms up understanding through creating logos to represent each value.

The last task gives students a chance to tell their stories and understand how families and people who care for them can create values. The partner has the important job of listening and hearing the story through the filter of human values.

These values will be reviewed later and students will be able to pick out the five that mean the most to them to create their own personal life logo.

What are the values for success in life?

VALUES – we all need them to be happy and live a life to be proud of

'Human values give respect to life and enhance happiness' *Human Values Foundation*

Values – such as honesty, kindness, love and forgiveness – can determine your behaviour and attitude. Have you thought about YOUR values?

First thoughts

What do you value?

Whom do you value?

What does our country value?

What do you believe in?

Values quiz – rate yourself 1–5 on each of these questions.

1 means you rate yourself low, 5 means very high.

1. I know what my values are.

2. My values help me decide what to do when I have problems.

3. I have opinions on most things.

4. I know what I want in life.

5. I know what my school values.

6. If someone asks me to do something that I don't feel is right, I say no.

Where do you get your values from?

What are the values for success in life?

Here are some values we are going to think about.

 V – Vote for democracy and equality

 **A** – Attitude is everything

 L – Love is all you need

 U – Understanding that family and friends matter!

 E – Enterprise and energy will make you successful

 S – Social intelligence – communicate with confidence

for

 L – Laughter and fun

 I – I can choose

 **F** – Forgiveness and Fairness

 **E** – Earn respect through Empathy

TASK

Copy out the box above and create a picture or a different logo to go with each.

What are the values for success in life?

Telling your story (in pairs)

Tell your story or life history and try to show where your values have come from. Your partner now has to use what they learned in your story and repeat to the class what your key values are and why you have them.

Values for Life

LESSON 43

V is for Vote

**Values for Success in Life –
Vote for democracy and equality**

As a key value of our society this lesson reinforces the democratic principles and explores reasons to vote. The link between freedom and democracy can be linked to many current news issues. Teachers are encouraged to make links with these issues in the lessons.

The main task is a group activity that considers how government money should be spent. The purpose of the task is to understand how the decisions that can change our lives are made by the people we vote for.

Each group could feed back to the whole group about their priorities and decisions. The impact of the learning can be measured by asking the question at the end.

teacher's notes

V is for Vote

Values for Success in Life – Vote for democracy and equality

First thoughts

What does democracy mean?

Think of 3 words that sum up democracy for you.

Make a list of everything you have ever voted for, from television shows to school elections.

Voting quiz

At what age can you vote in a local election?

_____

At what age can you vote in a general election?

_____

At what age can you vote in a TV poll?

_____

How did the Prime Minister get his job?

_____

Can you name any countries that don't vote for their leaders?

_____

Would you like to live in one of these countries? Why?

_____

V is for Vote

TASK

What happens … you decide!

Using the following list, complete Task 1 and Task 2.

TASK 1

Choose your top 6 priorities.

TASK 2

You have £1,000,000.

Assign it to your six priorities. Explain your decision to the class.

Activity	Order of priority	Amount (£)
Nuclear weapons		
New hospitals		
Computers for schools		
Bus services		
Funding for Africa		
Flood defences		
Road tolls		
Prison places		
Youth centres		
Free travel for under 16s		
Cancer Research Funds		
Higher Pensions		
Support for drug addicts		
More parks in cities		

V is for Vote

Can you now complete this sentence?

I should vote because

_____

_____

_____

_____

_____

_____

_____

_____

_____

_____

_____

_____

_____

_____

DEMOCRACY

Extension task

Is democracy always good?
Does democracy always
mean equality?

LESSON 44

A is for Attitude

**Values for Success in Life –
Attitude is everything**

The aim of this lesson is to help students
reflect on the messages they often
unconsciously convey.

After the first thoughts the task is to think
how to reframe the stereotypical teenage
attitude with an opposing viewpoint.

The self-assessment gives students an
opportunity to understand the way people are
judged in terms of attitude and actions.

The lesson then links up to how attitude
impacts on applications for jobs and in later
life. Creating the application creates a picture
of a different version of themselves with a very
positive attitude.

The message of this lesson is that attitude is
important and that the messages you give can
be changed.

A is for Attitude

Values for Success in Life – Attitude is everything

First thoughts

What do we mean by a bad attitude?

Am I bovvered?

What does it matter what YOU think?

Whatever!

What's your problem?

I really don't care!

A is for Attitude

Discuss the sort of situations when you think or say these statements. What messages are you giving? Why do teenagers act like this?

TASK

Redraw the bubbles with the OPPOSITE view inside them. Colour them in bright colours and draw an appropriate cartoon character.

Employers always stress the importance of attitude for success and career progression. What is a good attitude?

Reference written about an employee who works at a retail store.

Kevin has an attitude problem that affects everything he does and says. He has an unpleasant growl when spoken to and shrugs his shoulders when a customer asks for help. He often just doesn't take advice about how to do the job more effectively and doesn't seem to be listening even when being given important instructions on Health and Safety. He speaks only when spoken to and none of the team wants to work with him. I have had no alternative but to ask him to leave the business.

A is for Attitude

Write the job reference out again saying the opposite of all the comments that have been given about Kevin, thus describing someone with a very positive attitude.

What is <u>your</u> attitude – mark yourself 1–5 (1 is low, 5 is high)

I smile a lot

I greet people in the morning even if I don't know them well

I listen to other's views

I like to do a job well

I don't mind working hard

I like to impress people

I open doors for people or help them out

People who come into contact with me go away feeling happier

I am friendly to people I don't know

I try to use my initiative if I am stuck

I think it's important to keep learning

I am open to new ideas

Faking it to make it

Thinking about what you put into the table above, write yourself a letter of application to get your dream job. Really exaggerate your positive attitude. Work the sentences in the table above into your letter.

LESSON 45

L is for Love

Values for Success in Life – Love is all you need

A difficult value to teach but a crucial one for students to reflect on.

First thoughts – try to use the starter to explore different types of love. These could be discussed in pairs, then use class discussions to develop the thinking.

According to Wikipedia, '*Love is any of a number of emotions and experiences related to a sense of strong affection or profound oneness.*' They go on to say that there are the following categories of love:

- Historically – Courtly love

- Religious love

- Types of Emotion
  - Erotic love
  - Platonic love
  - Familial love
  - Puppy love
  - Romantic love.

Resources

It is suggested that a variety of poems about love are read out by the teacher and some rock/pop music and perhaps a rap about love are listened to.

Completing the sentences could be an easy way for students to create a poem about love.

The task asking the students to write an explanation to an alien about the concept of love makes the students think in quite an objective way what love means to humans.

teacher's notes

L is for Love

Values for Success in Life – Love is all you need

What is love?

'Love is an energy which flows from one to another… It is pure, giving and an unselfish experience. It is unconditional'   *Human Values Foundation*

Love changes everything … Money can't buy you love …

First thoughts

What does love mean to you?

I love football

I love you

I love chocolate

I love the beach

I love my mum

I love my mates

I love God

I love myself

Discuss the different types of love.

Artists, poets and musicians have always been fascinated by love…

'Love is not love that alters when it alteration finds' (Shakespeare)

'Love means never having to say you're sorry' (tagline from the film Love Story – 1970)

'All you need is love' (The Beatles)

Play some music with lyrics about love and read a selection of love poems.

Complete these sentences to show you can see the different types of love:

Love is

Love is

Love is

Love is

Love is

Love is

L is for Love

What does love feel like, look and sound like?

Do animals love?

Circle the 15 words that relate the most to love for you.

Exciting   Nervous   Soft

                                              Red
              Gentle
Black   Dangerous

                    Angry   Warm
Cold
                       Shivery
                                      Kind
              Worry
Generous
                              Selfless
              Selfish

Blue   Happy   Yellow

        Kind   Forgiving
                    Sorry

Sunshine   Resentful

                    Happy
Beauty   Safe

Fun   Responsibility   Hope

L is for Love

TASK

What things do you do that demonstrate love?

Is love a value that you would like to include in your top three? Why? Why not?

Task: Imagine an alien from another planet wants you to explain what is meant by love and why it is important to us here on Earth.

Write your explanation:

LESSON 46

U is for Understanding

**Values for Success in Life –
Understanding that family and friends
matter!**

This lesson explores the way family (or carers)
and friends can influence values.

The starter activity asks for examples of how
family and friends influence our characters
and values.

It is also worth remembering that values can
also be acquired through personal, religious,
cultural and educational experience, in
addition to social experience.

This lesson deliberately links to friends and
family to help students identify their support
structures and who matters to them socially
(and who socialises them). The first thoughts
may reveal conflicts between the two groups
(family and friends) that can be developed in
class discussion.

The tasks attempt to develop an
understanding of what is meant by real
friendship and how to give and receive it.

The final tasks develop an understanding of
possible conflict areas. Role-play can be used
to explore how to resolve those conflicts.

The golden rules task helps assess
understanding of the value of family and
friends.

U is for Understanding

Values for Success in Life – Understanding that family and friends matter!

First thoughts

How has your family influenced you?

How do your friends influence you?

Are there any areas of conflict between friends and family?

Which of the following qualities do you most appreciate in friends and family?

Loyalty	Discipline	Good looks	Cleverness	Coolness
Sense of humour	Generosity	Good listener	Musicality	Popularity
Time for you	Strength	Rich	Optimistic	Love

For family write out the words in red. For friends write out the words in blue.
Use both colours if these qualities are important for both family and friends.

Family	Friends

U is for Understanding

Write an advert for a best friend.

A friend that would make you happy and successful.

What qualities would he or she have?

Wanted: Best friend… 'must…

Wanted: Best friend

U is for Understanding

How can you be a better friend?

Write down five things you can do today.

How do you handle it when you fall out with someone?

Write a list of things families and friends fall out about.

Family	Friends

Golden Rules.

Create 5 golden rules for family harmony.

1. _____

2. _____

3. _____

4. _____

5. _____

Create 5 golden rules for friendship.

1. _____

2. _____

3. _____

4. _____

5. _____

Choose one of these examples.

Role-play the conflict and show two versions – a positive and negative outcome.

E is for Enterprise and Energy

Values for Success in Life – Enterprise and Energy

The aim of this lesson is to encourage risk-taking and creativity and to realise that this takes energy.

The starter activity creates role models that can be explored in discussion.

The Dragons' Den activity is based on the television programme where millionaire business people give real funding to new business ideas.

If the teachers can bring in other teachers, teaching assistants or, ideally, real business representatives to play the role of the Dragons instead of students, the lesson will be even more effective.

This activity is quite restricted by time so teachers can extend this to two lessons if students are enjoying it.

It is important for the teacher to draw together the learning from this exercise in this value.

The presentations are crucial and need to be delivered with conviction and energy if they are to secure the funds.

The extension activity encourages students to develop enterprise work outside of (or in) school for a good purpose.

teacher's notes

E is for Enterprise and Energy

Values for Success in Life – Enterprise and Energy

First thoughts

Think of three famous people who have enterprise and energy. Name them.

Enterprise means you are not scared to take a risk – you have courage and a willingness to do a difficult task – and can think of new and original solutions. You take the initiative; you do not wait for someone else to go first.

Energy means you are lively and enthusiastic about working hard for what you want.

What is the opposite of these?

Why will having both enterprise *and* energy make you unstoppable?

TASK

Dragons' Den

Vote for the 3–5 most enterprising and energetic people in the class to be the Dragons. The Dragons will work out their imaginary careers and prepare criteria for how they will judge each group's products.

In groups, invent a product to sell to the Dragons. (20 mins.)

Each Dragon has up to £50,000 to invest in each group.

Prepare a 3 minute presentation to make to the Dragons that will convince them to invest in your group.

The winning group will be the one that attracts the most investment.

The Dragons have to give positive feedback on how to be enterprising and energetic to all groups.

Extension task

Create a mini business that will raise money for your favourite charity.

LESSON 48

S is for Social intelligence

**Values for Success in Life –
Social intelligence**

Social intelligence – How to be popular, feel confident with people and be a great communicator.

This lesson explores the importance of how we communicate to others.

The focus is on how body language and voice tonality can create or break rapport.

The first thoughts get the students considering what makes an impact when they first meet someone. The conclusion drawn will be that impressions often convey much more than what you say and do.

The next section explores what body language is and how it creates its own messages. Teachers can model moods with body language and get students to read their mood from their faces and posture. Students have a chance to do this in the tasks too.

The mirroring and matching exercises are typical of the training delivered to sales people to get customer rapport and this will be interesting to students.

Practising the sales exercise will give students a chance to experience the impact of their body language. The idea is to become more aware of how body language can create rapport. It is worth reviewing this in other lessons.

teacher's notes

Section 3 • Values for success in life

S is for Social intelligence

Values for Success in Life – Social intelligence

How to be popular, feel confident with people and be a great communicator

Getting on with people – often called interpersonal intelligence – is one of the most important skills for life. However, much of what we do when we communicate is not in our conscious awareness and we may not realise the impression we are making on others.

First thoughts

When you first meet someone what do you notice about them?

How long does it take you to form an opinion about whether you like them or not?

What impression do YOU make? There are some people that are immediately likeable. So **how would you make sure that you are one.**

The chart below shows what is important about you to the person you are communicating to:

Vocal: HOW YOU SOUND. 38%
Volume, pitch, pace, intonation and energy

Visual: THE WAY YOU LOOK. 55%
Posture, gestures, facial expressions, eye contact and dress

Content: WHAT YOU SAY. Only 7%

Make the above into a diagram, pie chart or cartoon.

S is for Social intelligence

So **body language** matters more than what you say. Body language is made up of:

1.   Your facial expressions.

2.   How you stand or sit.

3.   Whether you can keep eye contact.

4.   Posture and gesture.

5.   How you shake hands.

Your body language is very important in making you feel confident.

Think of someone who is confident. Describe their body language. Draw some stick men to show confident and anxious body posture. Draw some facial expressions too.

S is for Social intelligence

Volunteer to walk into the room with anxious and confident body language and see how it makes you feel. What do other people recognise in your body language?

The way you walk and talk can make you feel differently too. When you feel worried you could change the way you feel by walking like your hero.

Positive body language also helps you get rapport with people you meet.

> Getting rapport is the key to making a great impact and being a confident communicator when you meet people.
>
> Rapport is 'a harmonious or sympathetic connection' with someone else. If you can get this then you will always make a good impression. To get rapport you need to 'tune' in to what others need and feel. Friends do this automatically. They match and mirror each other's behaviour and body language so that they feel comfortable with each other.

Talk in pairs about a holiday you would love to go on. Try to mirror each other's movements in a natural way and see how it feels.

TASK

Write out the actions from the list below that you think would help you get rapport.

Smile	Tilt your head sideways	Fold your arms	Turn your back	Slouch
Keep eye contact	Shoulders back	Frown	Raise your eyes to heaven	Speak clearly
Look down	Have your hair flop in your eyes	Head up	Laugh	Tut

TASK

Sell your pen to your neighbour – use rapport and mirroring to get rapport with your customer.

How did you describe it?

How much did you sell it for?

TOP TIP: From now on think about how you impact on others. Practise getting and breaking rapport and ask for feedback from people about how you come across to them.

LESSON 49

L is for Laughter and fun

**Values for Success in Life –
Laughter and fun**

A value that will be popular with students –
but how can you teach it?!

The purpose of this lesson is to convey the
message that laughing is good – especially if it
helps you take yourself less seriously. Also the
lesson raises awareness of the difference
between laughing with people and laughing at
them.

The starter gives time for reflection about
what makes us laugh and why.

Teachers can allow students to tell jokes in the
follow up discussion if they think what the
students can keep it clean, non-sexist and
non-racist!

The task that asks students to force
themselves to laugh to see if the chemistry in
their brain changes has been tried many times
by this author – with a very positive effect!!

Answering the problem page will allow
students to empathise with the victims of
mocking and try to imagine some solutions.

The plenary for this lesson is to test whether
students can accept that laughter and fun are
important, but the most important point is
that it's all right to laugh at your mistakes so
that you can move on.

L is for Laughter and fun

Values for Success in Life – Laughter and fun

First thoughts
Discuss your favourite comedy programmes and comedians. How do they make you laugh? Do they exaggerate body language? How often do you laugh? When was the last time and what caused it? Discuss with your neighbour.

LAUGHTER CHANGES YOUR BRAIN – try it. Make yourself laugh out loud and you will find it is contagious and you **really** will begin to laugh. This sparks the production of chemicals called endorphins in your brain that make you feel good.

What or who makes you laugh? _____

_____

How do you make others laugh? _____

_____

Why do some people laugh more often than others? _____

_____

Can you laugh at yourself? _____

_____

Why does alcohol make people giggle? _____

_____

Being able to laugh at yourself is a powerful way to boost your confidence and self-esteem because it enables you to laugh at mistakes and move forward.

L is for Laughter and fun

List some of your own and your family's funniest habits and share them with the group.

Can you make fun and laughter an important value in your life?

Tell a (clean) funny story to your neighbour – it can be made up or real.

In a group, share some jokes, and then analyse why they are funny.

Why do these things make us laugh?

★ Exaggeration
★ Falling over
★ Tickling
★ Teasing
★ Tricking others
★ Mistakes

L is for Laughter and fun

How do you feel when others laugh **at** you?

How can you make others laugh **with** you?

A teenager wrote the letter below to the problem page of a magazine.

Write a reply giving good advice on how to deal with the problems in future.

> Dear Jimbo,
>   Every time I'm out with my mates I seem to say something stupid and everyone laughs at me.
>   I've started to just keep quiet but some of them still make fun of me and I just don't know how to react. Help!!
>   Yours...
>   'Depressed'

Everybody loves a joker – or do they?

What does your neighbour think of the advice you gave and why?

Think of the jokes you know.

How many are hurtful in some way?

TOP TIPS: for getting **real** laughter into your life:
- Tell a joke which isn't hurtful
- Smile at someone today – make them feel good
- Make sure you laugh *with* people not *at* them
- Don't take yourself too seriously
- See the funny side of mistakes you make

LESSON 50

I is for I can choose

Values for Success in Life – I can choose

This lesson aims to make students more able to think about and, perhaps, resist peer pressure. They learn to do this by understanding how to develop a greater sense of personal power and responsibility.

Students explore the extent to which they are influenced by their peers in a way that promotes individual values as important. Students love their friends and they are often very powerful influences. However, have they thought about the impact they could have and the transient nature of teenage friendship?

The role-play should show the power that groups can have in making students commit crimes or act out of character and abandon their values. During the review of these role-plays it would be worth freezing the role-play and asking characters what is going through their mind at the moment they agree with or do something they know is wrong.

The final part of the lesson is about how easy it is to make excuses and play the victim. A reference to our litigious society could be developed here. Whose fault is it if we trip up and break a leg?

The powerful message to measure at the end is to make students realise that they always have a choice.

teacher's notes

I is for I can choose

Values for Success in Life – I can choose

This value is about your own personal power:

The power to forgive, the power to choose, the power to be happy, the power to manage your mind, the power to communicate…

But with power comes responsibility. Your greatest responsibility is to yourself.

Peer group pressure

How good are you at doing what *you* want?

Rate yourself (honestly) on how much you would be influenced by what others in your peer group think of the following:

First thoughts

Who influences you?

Give yourself 1 for very low influence and 5 for very high influence

1. The clothes you buy	
2. The music you listen to	
3. The friends you have	
4. Your hobbies and interests	
5. The lessons you like	
6. How hard you work at school	
7. The teachers you get on with	
8. Your attitude to your parents	
9. Your career ambitions	
10. How you spend your free time	
Total	**/ 50**

I is for I can choose

Who is in control of your life?

How can peer groups influence you in negative ways?

How can you be strong and stick to your values?

How many of your friends will still be your friends in ten years' time?
Describe the qualities of the friends who will still be around.

Create a group role-play that shows a group planning to commit a crime.
Show how members of the group can influence each other to do
things they would never do alone.

If it's to be it's up to me

I is for I can choose

Write down the 5s:

Write down five excuses for not doing your homework:

1. _____
2. _____
3. _____
4. _____
5. _____

Write down five excuses for not tidying your room:

1. _____
2. _____
3. _____
4. _____
5. _____

Write down five things you want in life:

1. _____
2. _____
3. _____
4. _____
5. _____

Write down five excuses for not getting them:

1. _____
2. _____
3. _____
4. _____
5. _____

Personal power means taking responsibility.

No excuses. No blaming others.

Just know you can make great choices.

'I CAN CHOOSE' – say that to yourself every day.

LESSON 51

F is for Forgiveness and Fairness

Values for Success in Life – Forgiveness and Fairness

Grudges grind you down.

The starter explores what forgiveness is and contrasts it with bearing grudges.

The emotions of anger and forgiveness can be explored through the tasks. The students can make up questions as an assessment of their understanding. The ability to make up 6 questions will test the extent to which they have developed their thinking. The answers to their questions can be discussed as a class or in groups.

As the lesson moves on to fairness it is suggested a Community of Enquiry approach is used (P4C).

This involves sitting in a circle and students speak one at a time on the topic – each one developing the thinking a little further with a statement or another question. The only rules are: One person speaks at a time, and all listen and support each other's right to their own view.

The extension task will require students to research Fair Trade for the next lesson to assess its purpose and value.

'Be the change you want to see in the world'.   *Ghandi*

teacher's notes

F is for Forgiveness and Fairnesss

Values for Success in Life – Forgiveness and Fairness

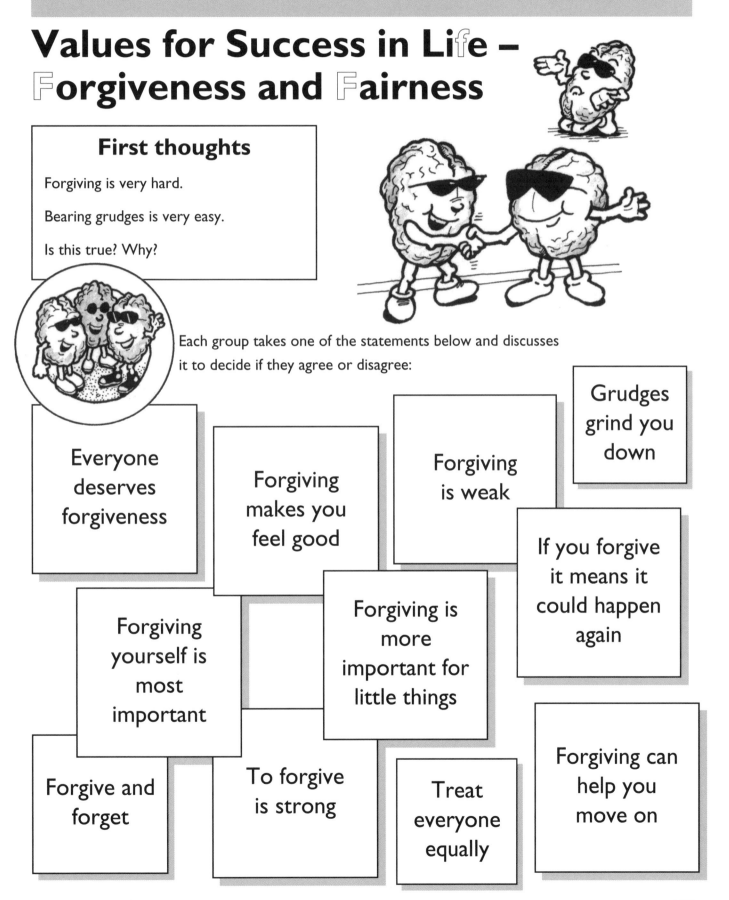

First thoughts

Forgiving is very hard.

Bearing grudges is very easy.

Is this true? Why?

Each group takes one of the statements below and discusses it to decide if they agree or disagree:

Grudges grind you down

Everyone deserves forgiveness

Forgiving makes you feel good

Forgiving is weak

If you forgive it means it could happen again

Forgiving yourself is most important

Forgiving is more important for little things

Forgive and forget

To forgive is strong

Treat everyone equally

Forgiving can help you move on

F is for Forgiveness and Fairness

Share what your group thought with the class.

What happens when you can't forgive and you bear a grudge? How do you feel? List your emotions.

Make up six questions about forgiveness such as:

How does it feel to forgive?

Why should I forgive?

1. _____
2. _____
3. _____
4. _____
5. _____
6. _____

Think of a real story about something that happened that made you feel angry. Write it down or tell it to your neighbour. Now answer each of your six questions and relate it to your story.

1. _____
2. _____
3. _____
4. _____
5. _____
6. _____

F is for Forgiveness and Fairness

Being fair means being able to weigh up what is right and wrong and to make a good decision.

You can't change what has happened but you can change how you feel about it.

Grudge is small and mean and angry.

Forgiveness is big and generous and kind.

Forgiveness and fairness go together.

'People will forget what you say, people will forget what you do but people will never forget how you made them feel.'

Is it fair that the food that you throw away in your bin could feed the starving families of Africa?

Can those families forgive you for throwing that good food away?

Extension task

Look up Fair Trade on the Internet and see what it means.

Hold a Community of Enquiry discussion in a circle about 'fairness'.

LESSON 52

E is for Earn respect through Empathy

**Values for Success in Life –
Earn Respect through Empathy**

For some students in recent years the word 'respect' has acquired a distorted meaning. This lesson aims to describe what respect truly means and to show how it relates to other values. For example, when students are shown how they can connect respect with empathy, they can begin to understand how to obtain and really earn respect.

This lesson is an opportunity to reinforce what respect means and how it relates to values. When we connect respect with empathy, we can help students understand how to earn respect as well as get it.

The starter considers who students respect and why. It is good to discuss the difference between respect and admiration when considering their heroes.

The rest of the lesson considers the importance of self-respect and good manners as part of the package of values in this section.

At the end students can be assessed by their choices for their personal shield. The personal shield gives students an opportunity to choose which aspects of respect matter to them and the links they have to their self-image.

The follow up task is to review the Values for Life section.
All the values can then be reviewed with a choice given to students to create their own values logo. This could be developed into a class values logo and put on the wall.

teacher's notes

E is for Earn respect through Empathy

Values for Success in Life – Earn respect through Empathy

Develop empathy to earn respect.

Empathy is the ability to put yourself into someone else's shoes. Empathy creates RESPECT for yourself and those around you.

First thoughts

Think of three people you respect and write their names below. Why do you respect them?

1 _____ 2 _____ 3 _____

_____

_____

_____

What actions make you respect yourself?

_____

_____

What actions make you respect someone else?

_____

_____

How can you earn respect from your friends?

_____

_____

E is for Earn respect through Empathy

Peer pressure

> Don't speak to him, no one likes him 'cos he's too boffy...

> You've got to have one of these - we all do...

> Haven't you got a boyfriend yet?

> Will they still like me if I don't stand up to him?

> Make up some more thought bubbles or speech bubbles that represent the dilemmas of self-respect versus group-respect.

What's the difference?

Good manners	Self-respect	Respect from others	Being polite

TASK

Create a personal shield that shows what respect means to you using pictures and words. Show your shield to the class and describe what it means.

VALUES Review task

Democracy and equality	Social communication
Attitude	Laughter and fun
Love	Personal responsibility
Friends and family	Forgiveness and fairness
Enterprise and energy	Empathy and respect

> From the ten VALUES you have discussed, choose your top five and create a logo around your name or nickname that weaves those values around you. Copy it and stick it on your books and belongings.

Glossary

Affirmations
Positive statements you say to yourself regularly to create self-belief.

Analytical thinking
Higher-order thinking that can break ideas down into parts or sequences.

Anchor
A word, gesture, sound, thought or movement that is linked to a particular state, which when 'fired' instantly activates that state again.

Attitude is everything
See Values for life.

Auditory learner
Someone who prefers to learn by listening. See Multisensory learning.

Body language
The messages created by facial expression, gestures, posture, positioning and so on, which can have a very powerful effect on communication.

Brain booster
A physical exercise which uses cross-lateral body movements to stimulate the brain. This is commonly known as *Brain Gym* (please see the Bibliography for more information).

Chunk your learning
Break the learning down into 20 minute lumps to make it accessible and digestible.

Community of Enquiry
A group discussion that begins with a stimulus and develops through questions into an enquiry where everyone takes part and contributes to a philosophical debate.

Competencies
Abilities and skills that can be developed to various levels. For example, learning to learn, self-discipline, resilience. Often used as an alternative to 'knowledge' taught in subjects.

Creative thinker
Someone who can generate many different ideas and novel solutions. Someone who explores ideas to see where they lead.

Earn respect through empathy
See Values for life.

Emotional brain
The part of the brain called the limbic system where memories are made and learning is most powerful.

Emotional Intelligence
This is knowing and understanding yourself well and having ways of thinking that make you self-confident and good at forming positive relationships with others. (Wikipedia: an ability, capacity or skill to perceive, assess and manage the emotions of one's self, others, and of groups.)

Empathy
Being able to see a situation from another person's point of view. (Wikipedia: one's ability to recognise, perceive and directly feel the emotion of another.)

Enterprise and energy will make you successful

See Values for life.

EQ

Emotional quotient (as opossed to Intelligence Quotient IQ). A way to express the measure of how high your emotional intelligence is. Also known as Emotional Intelligence.

Forgiveness and fairness

See Values for life.

I choose – personal power and responsibility

See Values for life.

Independent learning

Learning for yourself, by yourself.

Internal dialogue

The self-talk that takes place in every person's head as they pursue learning or any other conscious activity.

Interpersonal or People Smart

The ability to get on well with a wide range of other people and communicate effectively. See Multiple intelligences.

Intrapersonal or Self Smart

The ability to know your strengths and weaknesses, believe in yourself and motivate yourself to succeed. See Multiple intelligences.

Kinesthetic or Body Smart

The ability to develop physical skills and use them effectively in a variety of situations. See Multiple intelligences.

Kinesthetic learner

A learner who prefers hands-on experience and using physical activity when learning. See Multisensory learning.

L2L

Learning to Learn – the concept of learning how to learn effectively and transfer learning to a variety of contexts. This would include understanding how learning works for you as an individual, and developing flexible approaches to learning.

Laughter and fun

See Values for life.

Learning map

A diagram that shows the essential ideas and concepts in a topic in a structured pattern.

Learning to Learn

See L2L.

Life coach

Someone who can support the development of skills for life that create successful outcomes for individuals.

Limbic system

See Emotional brain.

Linguistic or Word smart

The ability to use written and spoken words effectively and communicate with skill and flexibility. See Multiple intelligences.

Love will make you happy

See Values for life.

Maps

See Pictorial learning map and learning map.

Match and mirror

Copy carefully the movements and body language of another.

Mathematical logical or Number smart

The ability to use numbers effectively in a variety of contexts See Multiple intelligences.

Metacognition

Standing back from thoughts and feelings and observing their impact. Thinking about thinking.

Mind movies

Pictures and images created in the mind, both constructed from past experience and created from future possibilities.

Mood control

Understanding that moods are a matter of choice that can be controlled and changed using certain strategies.

Mood monitor

A tool for taking control of moods or destructive thinking patterns.

Multiple intelligences

Howard Gardner's theory that suggests there are many ways to be clever. These are interpersonal, intrapersonal, linguistic, mathematical and logical, visual and spacial, physical and kinesthetic, musical and naturalist.

Multisensory learning

The notion that learning takes place through the senses, mainly the visual (sight), auditory (hearing) and kinesthetic (physical/ touch) senses. At different times some people have a stronger preferences for learning using one sense, but we all learn with all the senses and the best learning encompasses all three.

Musical or Music Smart

The ability to create and understand nuances of music. See Multiple intelligences.

Naturalist or Nature Smart

The ability to work effectively with and within nature, for example animals, agriculture, science and so on. See Multiple intelligences.

NLP

Neuro-linguistic programming – 'the users manual for the mind'. A philosophy that leads to a set of techniques to help develop the personal flexibility needed for success and happiness.

Open and closed questions

Open questions hand control to the person answering and require consideration to supply a long answer; for example, 'How do you feel?' Closed questions are those where the questioner retains control and have a short answer; for example, 'Are you happy?'

Optimism cake

The combination of ingredients that will create an optimistic outlook.

P.E.T. brain

The three part brain: Physical (reptilian), emotional, and thinking parts of the brain. Used to help students understand how and why they get angry, happy and clever.

Pictorial learning map

A way of representing connections and thinking in pictures and words to help with learning.

Rapport
Elegant communication through body language and speech that achieves a harmony between sender and receiver. This is achieved through high levels of empathy and highly developed listening skills.

Self-awareness
Knowing yourself well and responding to personal development challenges.

Smarts
These are shortened more student friendly versions of the words describing the multiple intelligences first presented by Howard Gardner as demonstrating there are many ways to be clever. See Multiple intelligences.

Social intelligence – communicate with confidence
See Values for life.

Stress buster
A technique to combat stress through self management.

Thinker
See Analytical and creative.

Thinking brain
The neo-cortex where the higher order thinking happens in the brain.

Thinking hats
Edward De Bono's method of helping us understand six different thinking perspectives.

Triune brain
Dr Paul Maclean's theory of the three-part brain, used to help students understand how to take control of their learning.

Understanding that family and friends matter
See Values for life.

VAK
Abbreviation for Visual, Auditory and Kinesthetic. Originally used in NLP theory to describe the seeing, hearing and feeling aspects of the structure of experience.

Values
Ideals and beliefs that are held by the individual, the group or society.

Values for life
Useful ideals and beliefs that can help with learning in the 21st century.

Visualisation
Creating and constructing visual images in the mind in a deliberate manner.

Visual learner
The ability to learn effectively through seeing, watching and creating visual images. See Multisensory learning.

Visual, Spatial or Picture Smart
The ability to have a sense of place and space as well as creative ability in the Arts. See Multiple intelligences.

Vote for democracy
See Values for life.

glossary

Bibliography

Auton J, (2004), *Education in Human Values*, Horsham, Human Values Foundation

Beere J, (2002), *The Key Stage 3 Learning Kit*, Lewes, Connect Publications

Beere J, (2005), *Creating the Learning School*, London, Paul Chapman

Bell N, (1991), *Visualizing and Verbalizing for Language Comprehension and Thinking*, San Luis Obispo, Gander Educational Publishing

Bosher M and Hazlewood P, (2006), *Nurturing Independent Thinkers*, Stafford, Network Educational Press

Claxton G, (1997), *Hare Brain, Tortoise Mind: why intelligence increases when you think less*, London, Fourth estate

Covey S, (1998), *The 7 Habits of Highly Effective Teenagers*, Arlington, Franklin

Davey S, (2004), *Unforgettable Places to See Before You Die*, BBC Books

De Bono E, (1985), *Six Thinking Hats*, New York, Little Brown & Co.

Dennison P E, & Dennison G E, (1989), *Brain Gym*, Ventura, Edu-Kinesthetics.

Gardner H, (1984), *Frames of Mind: The Theory of Multiple Intelligence*, London, Fontana

Gilbert I, (2002), *Essential Motivation in the Classroom*, Abingdon, RoutledgeFalmer

Goleman D, (1996), *Emotional Intelligence: why it can matter more than IQ*, London, Bloomsbury

Lucas, B, (2001), *Power Up Your Mind*, London, Nicholas Brearley Publishing

McClean P, (1990), *The Triune Brain in Evolution*, New York, Plenum

Merlevede P, (1997), *7 Steps to Emotional Intelligence*, Carmarthen, Crown House Publishing

Robbins A, (1992), *Awaken the Giant Within*, New York, Simon & Schuster

Rose C, (2000), *Master it Faster*, London, The Industrial Society

Rose C, & Nicholl M, (1997), *Accelerated Learning for the 21st Century*, New York, Delacorte Press

Smith A, (1998), *Accelerated Learning in the Classroom*, Stafford, Network Educational Press

Sperry R, (1968), *Hemisphere Disconnection and Unity in Conscious Awareness*, American Psychologist 23, 723–33

Index

The Independent Thinking Series brings together some of the most innovative practitioners working in education today under the guidance of Ian Gilbert, founder of Independent Thinking Ltd. www.independentthinking.co.uk

The Big Book of Independent Thinking: Do things no one does or do things everyone does in a way no one does — Edited by Ian Gilbert
ISBN 978-190442438-3

Little Owl's Book of Thinking: An Introduction to Thinking Skills — Ian Gilbert
ISBN 978-190442435-2

The Little Book of Thunks: 260 questions to make your brain go ouch! — Ian Gilbert
ISBN 978-184590062-5

The Buzz: A practical confidence builder for teenagers — David Hodgson
ISBN 978-190442481-9

Essential Motivation in the Classroom
ISBN 978-041526619-2

Are You Dropping the Baton?: How schools can work together to get transition right
— Dave Harris Edited by Ian Gilbert
ISBN 978-184590081-6

Leadership with a Moral Purpose: Turning Your School Inside Out — Will Ryan Edited by Ian Gilbert
ISBN 978-184590084-7

The Little Book of Big Stuff about the Brain — Andrew Curran Edited by Ian Gilbert
ISBN 978-184590085-4

Rocket Up Your Class!: 101 high impact activities to start, end and break up lessons —
Dave Keeling Edited by Ian Gilbert
ISBN 978-184590134-9

The Lazy Teacher's Handbook: How Your Students Learn More When You Teach Less —
Jim Smith Edited by Ian Gilbert
ISBN 978-184590289-6

The Learner's Toolkit: Developing Emotional Intelligence, Instilling Values for Life, Creating Independent Learners and Supporting the SEAL Framework for Secondary Schools —
Jackie Beere Edited by Ian Gilbert
ISBN 978-184590070-0

The Little Book of Charisma: Applying the Art and Science — David Hodgson Edited by Ian Gilbert
ISBN 978-184590293-3

The Little Book of Inspirational Teaching Activities: Bringing NLP into the Classroom —
David Hodgson Edited by Ian Gilbert
ISBN 978-184590136-3

The Little Book of Music for the Classroom: Using Music to Improve Memory, Motivation, Learning and Creativity — Nina Jackson Edited by Ian Gilbert
ISBN 978-184590091-5

The Little Book of Values: Educating children to become thinking, responsible and caring citizens — Julie Duckworth Edited by Ian Gilbert
ISBN 978-184590135-6

The Primary Learner's Toolkit: Implementing a creative curriculum through Cross Curricular Projects   Developing social and emotional intelligence   Creating independent, confident and lifelong learners — Jackie Beere Edited by Ian Gilbert
ISBN 978-184590395-4

www.independentthinking.co.uk   **www.crownhouse.co.uk**

The Competency Curriculum Toolkit

Developing the PLTS Framework Through Themed Learning

Jackie Beere and Helen Boyle

ISBN 978-184590126-4

This book explores the concept of a competency-based curriculum for KS3 and provides a range of resources for implementing creative learning in schools. It is widely acknowledged that students will need to be flexible, self-motivated learners if they are to thrive in our rapidly changing global community.

- Do students need to nurture their resilience and commitment to learning?
- Are schools keen to develop the skills and competencies of learning how to learn, leadership and teamwork ready for their crucial choices in KS4?
- Can we help students become more resilient and self reliant by teaching a project based approach that delivers progress in key personal competencies?

Various models for delivery and assessment are considered and schemes of work for projects as well as sample lessons to use in the classroom are provided. In addition, the CD-ROM has a range of PowerPoint presentations for training staff and students. An essential toolkit for all those wishing to develop independent learners.

The Primary Learner's Toolkit

Implementing a creative curriculum through Cross Curricular Projects: Developing social and emotional intelligence: Creating independent, confident and lifelong learners

Jackie Beere Edited by Ian Gilbert

ISBN 978-184590395-4

The Primary Learner's Toolkit is a companion to the best selling *The Learner's Toolkit* ISBN: 9781845900700. Here Jackie Beere does for Primary Teachers what The Learner's Toolkit did for Secondary Teachers. This is an essential resource for supporting the SEAL framework in primary schools and for all those teaching in primary schools. It contains everything you need to create truly independent learners, confident and resilient in their ability to learn and learn well. The book contains lessons plans and teachers notes and a CD-ROM in the back of the book has all the student forms and worksheets necessary for the lessons. Lessons include:

- getting to know yourself
- taking responsibility for your own life
- persistence and resilience
- setting goals for life
- controlling moods
- caring for your mind and body
- building brain power
- asking questions
- developing willpower
- pushing yourself out of your comfort zone
- prioritising and planning

The Learner's Toolkit Student Workbook 1

The Habits of Emotional Intelligence

The Learner's Toolkit Student Workbook 2

Lessons in Learning to Learn Values for Success in Life

Jackie Beere Edited by Ian Gilbert

ISBN 978-184590097-7

ISBN 978-184590103-5

To accompany *The Learner's Toolkit – Teacher's Resource*. These workbooks are designed for students to keep personal records of their work towards developing competencies in Learning, Emotional Intelligence and Values for Life. They are an outstanding resource for supporting the SEAL framework in secondary schools

Workbook 1 includes lessons on:

- Getting to know yourself
- Taking responsibility for your own life
- Building confidence
- Persistence and resilience
- Setting goals for life
- Controlling moods
- Caring for mind and body
- Optimism
- Stress Management
- Thinking Skills
- Communication and Cooperation

Workbook 2 Includes lessons on :

- How your brain works
- Multiple Intelligences
- How to use your senses for learning
- Democracy and equality
- Attitude
- Love and understanding
- Social Intelligence
- Forgiveness and fairness
- Empathy

Available as single copies or classroom packs – see www.crownhouse.co.uk for details